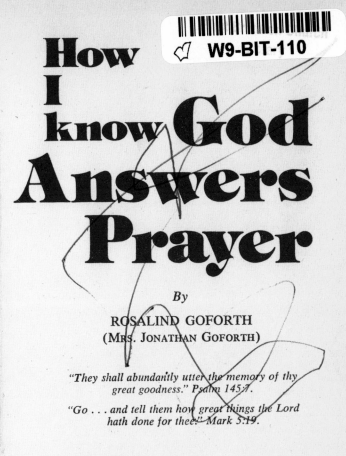

How I know God Answers Prayer

By

ROSALIND GOFORTH
(MRS. JONATHAN GOFORTH)

"They shall abundantly utter the memory of thy great goodness." Psalm 145:7.

"Go ... and tell them how great things the Lord hath done for thee." Mark 5:19.

WMS 2000-01

Bethel Publishing
Elkhart, IN

BETHEL
Publishing

Contents

Preface

It seems fitting that this little book of personal testimonies to answered prayer should have a brief introductory word as to how they came to be written. The question has been asked by some who read many of these testimonies as they appeared in the pages of *The Sunday School Times:* "How could you write such personal and sacred incidents in your life?" I could not have written them but for a very clear, God-given leading.

The story is as follows. When in Canada on our first furlough, I was frequently amazed at the incredulity expressed when definite testimony was given to an answer in prayer. Sometimes this was shown by an expressive shrug of the shoulders, sometimes by a sudden silence or turning of the topic of conversation, and sometimes more openly by the query: "How do you know that it might not have happened so anyway?"

Gradually the impression deepened. If they will not believe one, two, or a dozen testimonies, will they believe the combined testimonies of one whole life?

The more I thought of what it would mean to record the sacred incidents connected with answers to prayer, the more I shrank from the publicity and from undertaking the task. There were dozens of answers far too sacred for the public eye, which were known only to a few, others known only to God. But if the record were to carry weight with those who did not believe in the supernatural element in prayer, many personal and scarcely less sacred incidents must of necessity be made public.

Again and again I laid the matter aside as impossible. But I know now that the thing was of God. As months, even years, passed, the impelling sense that the record of answers to prayer *must* be written gave me no rest.

It was at the close of the 1908-10 furlough, during which, as a family, we had been blessed with many and — to our weak faith — wonderful answers to prayer, that my eldest son urged me to put down in some definite form the answers to prayer of my life and extracted from me a solemn promise that I would do so.

But months passed after returning to China, and the record had not been touched. Then came a sudden and serious illness which threatened my life, when the doctor told me I must not delay in getting my affairs in order.

It was then that an overwhelming sense of regret took possession of me that I had not set down the prayer testimonies, and solemnly I covenanted with the Lord that if He would raise me up they should be written.

There was no more question of what others might think; the one thought was to obey. The Lord raised me up; and although He had to deal with me very sternly once more before I really set

set myself to the task, the testimonies that are given here were written at last — most of them in odd moments of time during strenuous missionary journeys among the heathen.

Thus it will be seen that these incidents of answered prayer are not given as being more wonderful, or more worthy of record than multitudes the world over could testify to; but they are written and sent out simply and only because *I had to write them or disobey God.*

1

Getting Things from God

Are not five sparrows sold for two farthings, and not one of them is forgotten before God? . . . Fear not therefore: ye are of more value than many sparrows. LUKE 12:6-7

The pages of this book deal almost wholly with just one phase of prayer—petition. The record is almost entirely a personal testimony of what petition to my heavenly Father has meant in meeting the everyday crises of my life.

A prominent Christian worker, who read some of these testimonies in *The Sunday School Times,* said to me, "To emphasize getting things from God, as you do, is to make prayer too material."

To me this seems far from true. God is my Father; I am His child. As truly as I delight to be sought for by my child when he is cold, hungry, ill, or in need of protection, so is it with my heavenly Father.

Prayer has been hedged about with too many man-made rules. I am convinced that God has intended prayer to be as simple and natural and as constant a part of our spiritual life as the relationship between a child and his parent in the home. And as a large part of that relationship between child and parent is simply asking and receiving, just so is it with us and our heavenly Parent.

Perhaps, however, the most blessed element in this asking and getting from God lies in the strengthening of faith which comes when a definite request has been granted. What is more helpful and inspiring than a ringing testimony of what God has done?

As I have recalled the past in writing these incidents, one of the most precious memories is that of an evening when a number of friends had gathered in our home. The conversation turned to answered prayer. For more than two hours, we vied with one another in recounting personal incidents of God's wonderful work; and the inspiration of that evening still abides.

A Christian minister once said to me, "Is it possible that the great God of the universe, the Maker and Ruler of mankind, could or would, as you would make out, take interest in such a trifle as the trimming of a hat! To me it is preposterous!"

Yet did not our Lord Jesus Christ say, "The very hairs of your head are all numbered"; and "not one sparrow is forgotten before God"; and again, "Your heavenly Father knoweth what ye have need of *before* ye ask him"?

It is true that there is nothing too great for God's

power; and it is just as true that there is nothing too small for his love!

If we believe God's Word we must believe, as Dan Crawford has tersely and beautifully expressed it, "The God of the infinite is the God of the infinitesimal." Yes, He

> Who clears the grounding berg
> And guides the grinding floe,
> He hears the cry of the little kit fox
> And the lemming of the snow!

No more wonderful testimony, perhaps, has ever been given of God's willingness to help in every emergency of life than that which Mary Slessor gave, when asked to tell what prayer had meant to her. "My life," she wrote, "is one long daily, hourly record of answered prayer. For physical health, for mental overstrain, for guidance given marvelously, for errors and dangers averted, for enmity to the Gospel subdued, for food provided at the exact hour needed, for everything that goes to make up life and my poor service. I can testify, with a full and often wonder-stricken awe, that I believe God answers prayer. *I know God answers prayer!*"

I have been asked the question, "Has God *always* given you just what you have asked for?"

Oh, no! For Him to have done so would have been great unkindness. For instance, when I was a young woman I prayed for three years that God would grant me a certain petition. Sometimes I pleaded for this as for life itself, so intensely did I want it. Then God showed me very clearly that I was praying against His will. I resigned my will to His in the matter, and a few months later God gave what was infinitely better. I have often praised Him for denying my prayer; for had He granted it I could never have come to China.

Then too we must remember that many of our prayers, though always heard, are not granted because of some sin harbored in the life, or because of unbelief, or of failure to meet some other Bible-recorded condition governing prevailing prayer.

The following incidents of answered prayer are by no means a complete record. How could they be, when no record of prayer has been kept all these fifty years? Had there been, I doubt not that volumes could have been written to the glory of God's grace and power in answering prayer. But even from what is recorded here I too can say from a full heart, *I know God answers prayer*.

> He answered prayer: so sweetly that I stand
> Amid the blessing of His wondrous hand
> And marvel at the miracle I see,
> The favors that His love hath wrought for me.
> Pray on for the impossible, and dare
> Upon thy banner this brave motto bear,
>   "My Father answers prayer."

2

Early Lessons in the Life of Faith

I love the Lord, because he hath heard my voice and my supplications. PSALM 116:1

When a very little child, so young I can remember nothing earlier, a severe thunderstorm passed over our home. Terrified, I ran to my mother, who placed my hands together, and pointing upward repeated over and over again one word, *Jesus*.

More than fifty years have passed since that day, but the impression left upon my child-mind, of a Being invisible but able to hear and help, has never been effaced.

The most precious recollections of early childhood are associated with stories told us by our mother, many of which illustrated the power of prayer.

One that made an especially deep impression upon me was about our grandfather, who as a little boy went to visit cousins in the south of England, their home being situated close to a dense forest. One day the children, lured by the beautiful wild flowers, became hopelessly lost in the woods. After trying in vain to find a way out, the eldest, a young girl, called the frightened, crying little ones around her and said, "When Mother died, she told us to always tell Jesus if we were in any trouble. Let us kneel down and ask Him to take us home."

They knelt; and as she prayed, one of the little ones opened his eyes to find a bird so close to his hand that he reached out for it. The bird hopped away but kept so close to the child as to lead him on. Soon all were joining in the chase after the bird, which flew or hopped in front or just above and sometimes on the ground almost within reach. Then suddenly it flew into the air and away. The children looked up to find themselves on the edge of the woods and in sight of home.

With such influences bearing upon one at an impressionable age, it is not surprising that I came even as a very little child to just "tell Jesus" when in trouble.

Through the mists of memory one incident stands out clearly, which occurred when I was six or seven years of age. While playing one day in the garden, I was seized with what we then called "jumping" toothache. I ran to my mother for comfort, but nothing she could do seemed to ease the pain.

The nerve must have become exposed, for the pain was acute. Suddenly I thought, *Jesus can help me,* and just as I was, with my face pressed against my mother's breast, I said in my heart, *Lord Jesus, if You will take away this toothache right now,* now, *I will be Your little girl for three years.*

Before the prayer was fully uttered, the pain was entirely gone. I believe that Jesus had taken it away; and the result was that for years, when tempted to be naughty, I was afraid to do what I knew was wrong lest, if I broke my part of what I felt to be a pact, the toothache would return. This little incident had a real influence over my early life, gave me a constant sense of the reality of a divine presence, and so helped to prepare me for the public confession of Christ as my Saviour a few years later, at the age of eleven.

About a year after my confession of Christ, an incident occurred which greatly strengthened my faith, and led me to look to God as a Father in a new way.

When Easter Sunday morning came, it was so warm only spring clothes could be worn. My sister and I decided at breakfast that we would not go to church, as we had only our old winter dresses. Going to my room, I turned to my Bible to study it, when it opened at Matthew 6, and my eye rested on these words: "Why take ye thought for raiment? . . . Seek ye first the kingdom of God, and all these things shall be added unto you."

It was as if God spoke the words directly to me. I determined to go to church, even if I had to humiliate myself by going in my old winter dress. The Lord was true to His promise; I can still feel the power the resurrection messages had upon my heart that day so long ago. And further, on the following day a box came from a distant aunt, containing not only new dresses but much else that might well be included in the "all these things."

An unforgettable proof of God's loving care came to us as a family about this time, when my parents were face to face with a serious financial crisis. Isaiah 65:24 was literally fulfilled: "Before they call, I will answer; and while they are yet speaking, I will hear."

At that time, it is necessary to state, we depended on a quarterly income, which came through my mother's lawyer in England. Unusual circumstances had so drained our resources that we found ourselves in the middle of the quarter with barely sufficient to meet a week's needs. My dear mother assured us that the Lord would provide, that He would not forsake those who put their trust in Him. That very day a letter came from the lawyer in England, enclosing a draft for a sum ample to meet our needs till the regular remittance should arrive. This unexpected and timely draft proved to be a bonus, which did not occur again.

Some years later, having moved to a strange city, a great longing came to do some definite service for my Master. One day there came to the Bible class I attended a call for teachers to aid in a Sunday school nearby. When I presented myself before the superintendent and offered my services, it is not much wonder I received a rebuff, for I was young and quite unknown. I was told that if I wished a class, it would be well for me to find my own scholars. I can remember how a lump seemed choking me all the way home that day.

At last, determining not to be baffled, I prayed the Lord to help me get some scholars. I went forth, praying every step of the way, the following Saturday afternoon; and, canvassing just one short street near our home, I received the promise of nineteen children for Sunday school. The next day a rather victorious young woman walked up to the Sunday school superintendent with seventeen children following. Needless to say I was given a class.

In the autumn of 1885, the Toronto Mission Union, a faith mission, decided to establish a branch mission in the east end slums of that city. Three others and I were chosen to open this work. Everything connected with it was entirely new to me, but I found it most helpful and inspiring. For in face of tremendous difficulties, that seemed to my inexperienced eyes insurmountable, I learned that prayer was the secret which overcame every obstacle, the key that unlocked every closed door.

I felt like a child learning a new and wonderful lesson—as I saw benches, tables, chairs, stove, fuel, lamps, oil, even an organ coming in answer to definite prayer for these things. But best sight of all was when men and women, deep in sin, were converted and changed into workers for God, in answer to prayer. Praise God for the lessons then learned, which were invaluable later when facing the heathen.

The time came when two diverse paths lay before me—one to England, as an artist; one to China, as a missionary. Circumstances made a definite decision most difficult. I thought I had tried every means to find out God's will for me, and no light had come.

But in a day of great trouble, when my precious mother's very life seemed to hang in the balance, I shut myself up with God's Word, praying definitely for Him to guide me to some passage by which I might know His will for my life. My Bible, opening at John 15:16, seemed to bring a message to me: "Ye have not chosen me, but I have chosen you, and ordained you, that ye should go and bring forth fruit." Going to my dear mother and telling her of the message God had given me, she said, "I dare not fight against God."

From that time the last hindrance from going to China was removed. Surely the wonderful way God has kept His child for more than thirty years in China is proof that this call was not a mistaken one. "In all thy ways acknowledge him, and he will make plain thy paths" (Pr 3:6, ASV marg.).

During the summer of 1887 a book written by Dr. Hudson Taylor came into my hands. In *China's Spiritual Needs and Claims,* the writer told many instances of God's gracious provision in answer to prayer. The incidents related impressed me deeply. A little later, a few weeks before my marriage, when I found I was short fifty dollars of what I would need to be married free of debt, I resolved not to let others know of my need, but to just trust God to send it to me. The thought came, *If you cannot trust God for this, when Hudson Taylor could trust for so much more, are you worthy of being a missionary?*

It was my first experience of trusting quite alone for money. I was sorely tempted to give others just a hint of my need. But I was kept from doing so; and though I had a week or more of severe testing, peace of mind and the assurance that God would supply my need came at length. The answer, however, did not come till the very last night before the wedding.

That evening a number of my fellow workers from the East End Mission called and presented me with a beautifully illuminated gift, also a purse. After these friends had left I returned to my home circle, assembled in the back parlor, and showed them the gift and the purse unopened! Not for a moment did I think there was anything in the purse till my brother said, "You foolish girl, why don't you open it?" I opened the purse and found it contained a check for fifty dollars!

This incident has ever remained peculiarly precious; for it seemed to us a seal of God upon the new life opening before us.

3

"Go Forward On Your Knees"

(1887-1894)

I will go before thee, and make the crooked places straight: I will break in pieces the gates of brass, and cut in sunder the bars of iron.
ISAIAH 45:2

In attempting to record what prayer meant in our early pioneer days, other than purely personal testimonies must be given; for we were, as a little band of missionaries, bound together in our common needs and dangers by a very close bond.

In October 1887, my husband was appointed by the Canadian Presbyterian Church to open a new field in the northern section of the province of Honan, China. We left Canada the following January, reaching China in March 1888. Not until then did we realize the tremendous difficulties of the task before us.

Dr. Hudson Taylor, of the China Inland Mission, writing to us at this time, said,

We understand North Honan is to be your field; we, as a mission, have tried for ten years to enter that province from the south, and have only just succeeded. It is one of the most anti-foreign provinces in China. . . . Brother, if you would enter that province, *you must go forward on your knees*.

These words gave the keynote to our early pioneer years. Would that a faithful record had been kept of God's faithfulness in answering prayer! Our strength as a mission and as individuals, during those years so fraught with dangers and difficulties, lay in the fact that we did realize the hopelessness of our task apart from divine aid.

The following incident occurred while we were still outside Honan, studying the language at a sister mission. It illustrates the importance of prayer from the home base for those on the field.

My husband was finding great difficulty in acquiring the language; he studied faithfully many hours daily but made painfully slow progress. He and his colleague went regularly together to the street chapel to practice preaching in Chinese to the people; but, though Mr. Goforth had come to China almost a year before the other missionary, the people would ask the latter to speak instead of my husband, saying they understood him better.

One day, just before starting as usual for the chapel, my husband said, "If the Lord does not give me very special help in this language, I fear I shall be a failure as a missionary."

Some hours later he returned, his face beaming with joy. He told me that he realized most unusual help when his turn came to speak; sentences came to his mind as never before; and not only had he made himself understood, but some had appeared much moved, coming up afterward to have further conversation with him. So delighted and encouraged was he with this experience that he made a careful note of it in his diary.

Some two months and a half later, a letter came from a student in Knox College, saying that on a certain evening a number of students had met specially to pray for Mr. Goforth. The power of prayer was such and the presence of God so manifestly felt, that they decided to write and ask Mr. Goforth if any special help had come to him at that time. Looking in his diary, he found that the time of their meeting corresponded with that time of special help in the language.

I cannot tell why there should come to me
    A thought of someone miles and years away,
In swift insistence on the memory,
    Unless there is a need that I should pray.
We are too busy to spare thought
    For days together of some friends away;
Perhaps God does it for us — and we ought
    To read His signal as a sign to pray.
Perhaps just then my friend has fiercer fight,
    A more appalling weakness, a decay
Of courage, darkness, some lost sense of right;
    And so, in case he needs my prayers—I pray.

At last the joyful news reached us women, waiting outside of Honan, that our brethren had secured property in two centers. It would be difficult for those in the homeland to understand what the years of waiting had meant to some of us. The danger to those dear to us, touring in Honan, was very great. For years they never left us to go on a tour without our being filled with dread lest they should never return; yet the Lord, in His mercy, heard our prayers for them; and though often in grave danger, none received serious injury. This is not a history of the mission, but I cannot forbear giving here one incident illustrating how they were kept during those early days.

Two of our brethren, after renting property at a town just within the boundary of Honan, and near the Wei River, moved in, intending to spend the winter there; but a sudden and bitter persecution arose just as they had become settled. The mission premises were attacked by a mob, and everything was looted. The two men were roughly handled, one being dragged about the courtyard. They found themselves at last left alone, their lives spared, but everything gone.

Their position was serious in the extreme—several day's journey away from friends, with no money, no bedding, and no clothes but those upon them, and the cold winter begun.

In their extremity, they knelt down and committed themselves to the Lord. And according to His promise He delivered them out of their distresses; for even while they prayed a brother missionary from a distant station was at hand. He arrived unexpectedly, without knowing what had occurred, a few hours after the looting had taken place. His coming at such an opportune moment filled the hearts of their heathen enemies with fear. Money and goods were returned, and from that time the violent opposition of the people ceased.

A few months after the above incident, several families moved into Honan, and a permanent occupation was effected; but the hearts of the people seemed as adamant against us. They hated and distrusted us as if we were their worst enemies. The district in which we settled was known for its turbulent and antiforeign spirit, and as a band of missionaries we were frequently in the gravest danger.

Many times we realized that we, as well as our fellow workers at the other stations, were kept from serious harm only by the overruling, protecting power of God in answer to the many prayers which were going up for us all at this critical juncture in the history of our mission. The following are concrete examples of how God heard our prayers at this time.

We had for our station doctor a man of splendid gifts. He was a gold medalist, with years of special training and hospital experience, and was looked upon as one of the rising physicians in the city from which he came. Imagine his disappointment, therefore, when month after month passed and scarcely a good case came to the hospital. The people did not know what he could do, and moreover they were afraid to trust themselves into his hands. We, as a little band of missionaries, began to pray definitely that the Lord would send cases to the hospital which would open the hearts of the people toward us and our message.

It was not long before we saw this prayer answered beyond all expectation. Several very important cases came almost together, one so serious that the doctor hesitated for days before operating. When at last the operation did take place the doctor's hands were strengthened by our prayers, the patient came through safely, and a few days later was going around a living wonder to the people.

Very much depended upon the outcome of this and other serious operations. Had the patients died under the doctor's hands, it would have been quite sufficient to have caused the destruction of the mission premises and the life of every missionary. Three years later the hospital records showed that there had been 28,000 treatments in one year.

Again, we kept praying that the Lord would give us converts from the very beginning. We had heard of missionaries in India, China, and elsewhere, who had worked for many years without gaining converts; but we did not believe that this was God's will for us. We believed that it was His pleasure and purpose to save men and women through His human channels, and why not from the beginning? So we kept praying and working and expecting converts, and God gave them to us. The experience of thirty years has confirmed this belief.

Space permits the mention of but two of these earliest converts.

The first was Wang Feng-ao, who came with us into Honan as my husband's personal teacher. He was a man of high degree, equal to the Western M.A., and was one of the proudest and most overbearing of Confucian scholars. He despised the missionaries and their teaching, and so great was his opposition that he would beat his wife every time she came to see us or listen to our message. But Mr. Goforth kept praying for this man and using all his influence to win him for Christ.

Before many months passed a great change had come over Mr. Wang; his proud, overbearing manner had changed, and he became a humble, devout follower of the lowly Nazarene. God used a dream to awaken this man's conscience, as it not uncommon in China. One night he dreamed he was struggling in a deep, miry pit; but try as he would he could find no way to escape. When about to give up in despair, he looked up and saw Mr. Goforth and another missionary on the bank above him, with their hands stretched out to save him. Again he sought for some other way of escape; but finding none, he allowed them to draw him up.

This man, later on, became my husband's most valued evangelist. For many years his splendid gifts were used to the glory of his Master in the work among the scholar class in the Changtefu district. He has long since passed to his reward, dying as he had lived, trusting only in the merit of Jesus Christ for salvation.

Another of the bright glints in the darkness of those earliest days in Honan was the remarkable conversion of Wang Fu-Lin. For many years his business had been that of a public storyteller; but when Mr. Goforth came across him, he was reduced to an utter wreck through opium smoking. He accepted the Gospel, but for a long time seemed too weak to break off the opium habit. Again and again he tried to do so, but failed hopelessly each time.

The poor fellow seemed almost past hope, when one day my husband brought him to the mission in his cart. The ten days that followed can never be forgotten by those who watched Wang Fu-Lin struggle for physical and spiritual life. I believe nothing but prayer could have brought him through. At the end of the ten days the power of opium was broken, and Wang Fu-Lin came out of the struggle a new man in Jesus Christ.

I shall have occasion to speak of this man again.

In all the cases of divine healing cited in this record, it will be noted that God healed in answer to prayer either when the doctors had done all in their power and hope had been abandoned, or when we were out of reach of medical aid.

Soon after coming to China the Reverend Hunter Corbett, one of the most devoted and saintly of God's missionaries, gave a testimony which later was used of God to save me from giving up service in China and returning home to Canada.

Dr. Corbett said that for fifteen years he had been laid aside every year with that terrible scourge

25

of the East—dysentery; and the doctors at last gave a definite decision that he must return at once to the homeland and forsake China. "But," said the grand old man, "I knew God had called me to China, and I also knew that God did not change. So what could I do? I dared not go back on my call; so I determined that if I could not live in China I could die there; and from that time the disease lost its hold on me."

This testimony was given over twenty-five years ago, when he had been almost thirty years in China! In January 1920, when well-nigh ninety years of age, this beloved and honored saint of God passed to higher service.

For several years I had been affected just as Dr. Corbett had been, and each year the terrible disease seemed to be getting a firmer hold upon me. At last, one day my husband brought me the decision of the doctors, that I should return home. And as I lay there ill and weak, the temptation to yield came. But, as I remembered Dr. Corbett's testimony, and my own clear call, I felt that to go back would be to go against my own conscience. I therefore determined to do as Dr. Corbett had done—leave myself in the Lord's hands—whether for life or for death. This happened more than twenty years ago, and since then I have had very little trouble from that dread disease.

Yes, the deeper the need, and the bitterer the extremity, the greater the opportunity for God to show forth His mighty power in our lives, if we but give Him a chance by unswerving obedience at any cost. "In the day when I cried thou answeredst me, and strengthenedst me with strength in my soul" (Ps 138:3).

During our fourth year in China, when we were spending the hot season at the coast, our little son, eighteen months old, was taken very ill with dysentery. After several days' fight for the child's life, there came the realization one evening that the angel of death was at hand.

My whole soul rebelled; I actually seemed to hate God; I could see nothing but cruel injustice in it all; and the child seemed to be going fast. My husband and I knelt down beside the little one's bedside, and he pleaded earnestly with me to yield my will and my child to God. After a long and bitter struggle, God gained the victory, and I told my husband I would give my child to the Lord. Then my husband prayed, committing the precious soul into the Lord's keeping.

While he was praying, I noticed that the rapid, hard breathing of the child had ceased. Thinking my darling was gone, I hastened for a light, for it was dark; but on examining the child's face I found that he had sunk into a deep, sound, natural sleep, which lasted most of the night. The following day he was practically well of the dysentery.

To me it has always seemed that the Lord tested me to almost the last moment; then, when I yielded my dearest treasure to him and put my Lord first, He gave back the child.

While writing the above, I came across an extract from the *Christian* of March 12, 1914, in which the editor said,

> Speaking at the annual meeting of the Huntingdon County Hospital, Lord Sandwich referred to the power of spiritual healing, and premising that the finite mind cannot measure the power of the infinite, said he "looked forward to the day when the spiritual doctrine of healing and the physical discoveries of science will blend in harmonious combination, to the glory of God and the benefit of humanity.

4

A God-Given Field (1894-1900)

Lord, there is none beside thee to help, between the mighty and him that hath no strength; help us, O Lord our God; for we rely on thee, and in thy name are come against this multitude.
2 CHRONICLES 14:11

The story of the opening of Changte is so connected by a chain of prayer that to give isolated instances of prayer would be to break the chain.

A few months after our arrival in China an old, experienced missionary kindly volunteered to conduct Mr. Goforth and his colleague, who had just arrived, through North Honan, that they might see the field for themselves.

Traveling southward by cart, they crossed the border into Honan early one morning. As my husband walked beside the carts that morning, he felt led to pray that the Lord would give that section of Honan to him as his field. The assurance came that his prayer was granted. Opening his daily textbook, he found the passage for that morning was from

Isaiah 55:8-13. Like a precious promise of future blessing for that field came the words: "As the rain cometh down, and the snow from heaven, and returneth not thither, but watereth the earth, and maketh it bring forth and bud, that it may give seed to the sower, and bread to the eater: so shall my word be that goeth forth out of my mouth: it shall not return unto me void."

For six years, however, our faith was sorely tested.

Of all places, Changte seemed most determined to keep out the missionary. And there were other difficulties in the way. A presbytery had been formed as others joined us, and all matters had to be decided by that body. Two stations that had been opened, where a foothold could first be gained, required all, and more than all, the force we then had. So for six years the door to Changte remained fast closed. But during all those years, my husband never once lost sight of God's promise to him nor failed to believe it.

Again and again, when Mr. Goforth and his colleague visited the city, they were mobbed and threatened, the people showing the utmost hostility. But the day came, at last, when the long-prayed-for permission from the presbytery to open Changte was granted. The very next morning found Mr. Goforth en route for Changte to secure property for a mission site. Often has he told how, all the way over that day to Changte, he prayed the Lord to open the hearts of the people, and make them willing to give him the property most suitable for the work. Within three days of his reaching Changte he had thirty-five offers of property, and was able to secure the very piece of land he had earlier chosen as most ideal for the mission.

Thus the Lord did break in pieces the gates of brass which had kept us so long from our promised land.

A year later I joined my husband there, with our three little children. It was arranged that our colleague should take charge of the outside evangelism, while we opened work at the main station.

To understand what it meant for us to have our need supplied, there should be some knowledge of what that need was.

We decided from the first that no one should be turned from our doors. Mr. Goforth received the men in the front guest room, while the women and children came to our private quarters. During those first weeks and months hundreds and thousands crowded to see us. Day by day we were literally besieged. Even at mealtime our windows were banked with faces.

The questions ever before us those days were, how to make the most of this wonderful opportunity, which would never come again after the period of curiosity was past; how to win the friendship of this people who showed in a hundred ways their hatred and distrust of us; how to reach their hearts with our wonderful message of a Saviour's love?

All that was in our power was to do, day by day, what we could with the strength that was given us.

From early morning till dark, sometimes nine or ten hours a day, the strain of receiving and preaching to these crowds was kept up. My husband had numbers of workmen to oversee, material for building to purchase, and to see to all the hundred and one things so necessary in building up a new station. Besides all this he had to receive and preach to the crowds that came. He had no evangelist, Mr. Wang being then lent to another missionary. I had my three little children and no nurse or Bible woman. When too exhausted to speak longer to the courtyard of women, I would send for my husband, who though tired out would speak in my stead. Then we would rest ourselves and entertain the crowd by singing a hymn.

So the days passed. But we soon realized that help must come, or we would both break down.

One day Mr. Goforth came to me with his Bible open at the promise, "My God shall supply all your need," and asked: "Do we believe this? If we do, then God can and will supply us with someone to help preach to these crowds, if we ask in faith."

He prayed very definitely for a man to preach. With my doubt-blinded heart, I thought it was as if he were asking for rain from a clear sky. Yet, even while he prayed, God was moving one to come to us. A day or two later there appeared at the mission the converted opium fiend, Wang Fu-Lin, whose conversion has been already recorded.

No one could have looked less like the answer to our prayers than he did. Fearfully emaciated from long years of excessive opium smoking, racked with a cough which three years later ended his life, dressed in such filthy rags as only a beggar would wear, he presented a pitiable sight. Yet the Lord seeth not as man seeth.

After consulting together, Mr. Goforth decided to try him for a few days, believing that he could at least testify to the power of God to save a man from his opium. Soon he was reclothed in some of my husband's Chinese garments; and within an hour or two of his entering the mission gate, practically a beggar, he was seated in charge of the men's chapel, so changed one could scarcely have recognized him.

From the first day of his ministry at Changte there was no doubt in the minds of any who heard him that he had indeed been sent to us by our gracious God, for he had in a remarkable degree the unction and power of the Holy Ghost. His gifts as a speaker were all consecrated to one object—the winning of souls to Jesus Christ. He seemed conscious that his days were few and always spoke as a dying man to dying men. Little wonder is it, therefore, that from the very beginning of his ministry in our chapel men were won to Christ. God spared him to us for the foundation laying of the church at Changte, then called him higher.

Mr. Goforth's need was relieved by the coming of Wang Fu-Lin, but not mine. The remarkable way God had sent him, however, gave me courage and faith to trust God to give me a Bible woman. Those who know anything of mission work in China will agree with me that it is far more difficult to find women than men who are able to preach the Gospel, or if able, who are free for the work. But I was beginning to learn that God is limited only from the human side and that He was always willing to give beyond our asking, if the human conditions He has so plainly laid down in His Word are fulfilled.

A short time after I had begun to ask my heavenly Father definitely for a Bible woman, one of the missionaries came in from a tour; and his first words were, "Well, Mrs. Goforth, I believe we have a readymade Bible woman for you!"

Then he told me how he had come across a widow and her son in a mountain village, who had heard the Gospel from a recent convert out of one of the other stations. This man had been a member of the same religious sect as the widow and her son. When he found Christ he at once thought of his friends and went over the mountain to tell them. Mrs. Chang received the Gospel gladly. She had been a preacher in that heathen sect and had gained the fluency in speaking and power in holding audiences so necessary in the preaching of the Gospel.

The way was soon opened for her to come to me, and she became my constant companion and valuable assistant in the women's work during those early years. She witnessed a good confession in 1900—being strung up by her thumbs when refusing to deny her Lord. Faithfully she served the Lord as a Bible woman, until the time of her death in 1903.

During the first two or three years at Chang Te

Fu we lived in unhealthy Chinese houses, which were low and damp. It was therefore thought best that we should have a good semiforeign house built for us. The work at this time was so encouraging— converts being added weekly, and sometimes almost daily—that we feared lest the new house would hinder the work and become a separating barrier between ourselves and the people. We therefore prayed that God would make the new house a means of reaching the people—a blessing, and not a hindrance. The answer to this prayer, as is often the case, depended largely upon ourselves. We had to be made willing to pay the price that the answer demanded.

In other words, we came to see that in order that our prayer could be answered we would have to keep open house every day and all day, which was by no means easy. Some assured us it was wrong, because it would make us cheap in the eyes of the Chinese; others said it was wrong because of the danger of infection to the children. But time proved these objections to be unfounded. The very highest as well as the lowest were received, and their friendship won by this means. And, so far as I can remember, our children never met any contagion because of this way of receiving the people into our house.

The climax in numbers was reached in the spring of 1899, when 1,835 men and several hundred women were received by us in one day. These were first preached to in large bands and then led through the house. We have seen evidences of the good of this plan in all parts of our field. It opened the hearts of the people toward us, and helped us to live down suspicion and distrust as nothing else could have done.

In May 1898, we started down to Tientsin by houseboat with our children for a much-needed rest and change. Cold, wet weather soon set in. Twelve days later, as we came in sight of Tientsin, with a bitter north wind blowing, our eldest child went on deck without his overcoat, in disobedience to my orders. Shortly after, the child came in with a violent chill. That afternoon, when we arrived in Tientsin, the doctor pronounced the verdict—pneumonia.

The following day, shortly after noon, a second doctor, who had been called in consultation, met a friend on his way from our boy's bedside and told her he did not think the child could live till morning. I had taken his temperature, and found it to be 106. He was extremely restless, tossing in the burning fever. Sitting down beside him, with a cry to the Lord to help me, I said distinctly, "Paul, you disobeyed me, and have thus brought this illness upon yourself. I forgive you; ask Jesus to forgive you, and give yourself to Him."

The child looked at me for a moment steadily then closed his eyes. I saw his lips move for a moment; then quietly he sank into a sound sleep. When he awoke, about dusk, I took his temperature, and found it 101. By the time the doctor returned, it was normal and did not rise again. Although he had been having hemorrhage from the lungs, this ceased.

Is not Jesus Christ the same yesterday, today, and forever? Why should we wonder, therefore, at His healing touch in this age? "According to your faith be it unto you."

During those early pioneer years, when laying the foundation of the Changte church, my own weak faith was often rebuked when I saw the results of the simple, childlike faith of our Chinese Christians. Some of those answers to prayer were of such an extraordinary character that, when told in the homeland, even ministers expressed doubts as to their genuineness. But, praise God, I know they are true. Here are two concrete examples.

Li-ming, a warmhearted, earnest evangelist, owned land some miles north of Chang Te Fu. On one occasion, when visiting the place, he found the neighbors all busy placing around their fields little sticks with tiny flags. They believed this would keep the locusts from eating their grain. All urged Li-ming to do the same and to worship the locust god, or his grain would be destroyed. Li-ming replied, "I worship the only true God, and I will pray Him to keep my grain, that you may know that He only is God."

The locusts came and ate on all sides of Li-ming's grain, but did not touch his. When my husband heard this story, he determined to get further proof, so he visited the place for himself and inquired of Li-ming's neighbors what they knew of the matter.

One and all testified that, when the locusts came, their grain was eaten and Li-ming's was not.

The Lord Jesus once said, after a conflict with unbelief and hypocrisy, "I thank thee, O Father, Lord of heaven and earth, because thou hast hid these things from the wise and prudent, and hast revealed them unto babes."

Our little Gracie became ill with a fatal disease, so common in malarious districts—enlarged spleen. The doctors pronounced her condition quite hopeless. One day a Chinese Christian woman came in with her little child, about the same age as our Gracie, and very ill with the same disease. The poor mother was in great distress, for the doctor had told her also that there was no hope. She thought that if we would plead with the doctor he could save her child. At last my husband pointed to our little Gracie, saying: "Surely, if the doctor cannot save our child, neither can he save yours; your only hope and ours is in the Lord Himself."

The mother was a poor, hard-working, ignorant woman, but she had the simple faith of a little child. Some weeks later she called again and told me the following story:

"When the pastor told me my only hope was in the Lord, I believed him. When I reached home I called my husband, and together we committed our child into the Lord's hands. I felt perfectly sure the child would get well, so I did not take more care of him than of a well child. In about two weeks he seemed so perfectly well that I took him to the doctor again, and the doctor said that he could discover nothing the matter with him."

That Chinese child is now a grownup, healthy man. And *our child died*. Yet we had prayed for her as few, perhaps, have prayed for any child. Why, then, was she not spared? I do not know. But I do know that there was in my life, at that time, the sin of bitterness toward another, and an unwillingness to forgive a wrong. This was quite sufficient to hinder any prayer, and did hinder for years, until it was set right.

Does this case of unanswered prayer shake my faith in God's willingness and power to answer prayer? No, no! My own child might just as reasonably decide never again to come to me with a request because I have, in my superior wisdom, denied a petition. Is it not true, in our human relationships with our children, that we see best to grant at one time what we withhold at another? "What I do thou knowest not now, but thou shalt know hereafter."

And one of the most precious experiences of God's loving mercy came to me in connection with our little Gracie's death. We had been warned that the end would probably come in convulsions; two of our dear children had been so taken. Only a mother who has gone through such an experience can fully understand the horror of the possibility that such might come again at any time.

One evening I was watching beside our little one, a friend being with me, when suddenly the child said very decidedly, "Call Papa; I want to see Papa." I hesitated to rouse her father, as it was his time to rest; so I tried to put her off with some excuse; but again she repeated her request, and so I called her father, asking him to walk up and down with her until I returned.

Going into the next room I cried in an agony to the Lord not to let Gracie suffer; but, if it was indeed His will to take the child, then to do so without her suffering. As I prayed, a wonderful peace came over me; and the promise came so clearly it was as if spoken: "Before they call I will answer; and while they are yet speaking I will hear." Rising, I was met at the door by my friend, who said, "Gracie is with Jesus." While I was on my knees, our beloved child, after resting a few moments in her father's arms, had looked into his face with one of her loveliest smiles, and then quietly closed her eyes and had ceased to breathe. No struggle, no pain, but a "falling on sleep."

"Like as a father pitieth . . . so the Lord pitieth."

Ever-darkening clouds gathered about us during the months following Gracie's death; and while the storm did not burst in all its fury till the early summer of 1900, yet the preceding winter was full of forebodings and constant alarms.

On one occasion thousands gathered inside and outside our mission, evidently bent on serious mischief. My husband and his colleagues moved in and out all that day among the dense crowd which filled the front courtyards, while we women remained shut within closed houses, not knowing what moment the mob would break loose and destroy us all.

What kept them back that day? What but trustful prayer! And the Lord heard prayer that day and wonderfully restrained the violence of our enemies.

We did not know then, but those experiences were preparing us for the greater trials and perils awaiting us all.

5

Our Deliverance from the Boxers (1900)

God is unto us a God of deliverances. PSALM 68:20 (ASV)
Who delivered us out of so great a death, and will deliver: on whom we have set our hope that he will also still deliver. 2 CORINTHIANS 1:10 (ASV)

Many times we were asked in the homeland to tell the story of our escape during the Boxer uprising, and often the question was put, "If it was really God's power that saved you and others on that journey, then why did He not save those of His children who were so cruelly put to death?"

For a time this question troubled me. Why indeed? One day when seeking for light on the matter I was directed to Acts 12. There I found the only answer that can be given. We are told in verse 2 that James was put to death by the sword; then the rest of the chapter is given to the detailed record of Peter's wonderful deliverance in answer to prayer (vv. 5, 12). In that day when all things shall be revealed I am convinced we shall see that *prayer* had much to do in the working out of our deliverance. When the first cable was received in Canada informing the home church of our party starting on that perilous journey, we were told a great wave of prayer went up for us from Christians of all denominations. The Presbyterian Assembly of Canada was meeting at the time, and one session was given entirely to prayer on behalf of the missionaries in China. Never had that body witnessed such a season of intense, united intercession.

Later in the homeland, when giving the story of our escape, repeatedly we have had people come to us telling how, during the weeks which elapsed between the first cable informing the home church of our danger, and the second cable, which told of our safe arrival at the coast, they had never ceased to cry to God to save us. Then too after all is said, we must believe God was glorified and God's purposes were fulfilled in the death of some as in the saved lives of others. The blood of the martyrs is still the seed of the Church.

It was in the month of June 1895, that an incident occurred which has ever been linked in my mind with the events of 1900. I was about to leave Toronto with my four children to join my husband in China, when a cable was received telling of the cruel massacre of Mr. and Mrs. Stewart and others. Deep and widespread sympathy was expressed and much anxiety felt for missionaries generally in

China. Many urged me to delay our return; but I felt it best to keep to our original plans, and a few days later found us bidding farewell to friends at the Union Station, Toronto.

Just as the train was leaving, a lady stepped forward quickly to the window and said, "You do not know me, but I have prayed the Lord to give me a promise for you; it is this, take it as from Him," and handed me a slip of paper. I opened the paper and read, "No weapon that is formed against thee shall prosper" (Is 54:17). Then and there I raised my heart to God in prayer that He would fulfill this promise to me and those dear to me; and as I prayed there came the clear assurance that the Lord heard.

Never can we forget that winter of 1899-1900. The clouds had begun to gather, and the mutterings of the coming storm were heard on all sides of us. Repeatedly we were as a mission in gravest danger, and at such times were literally "shut up to God." The temper of the people was such that any little thing angering them would have been as a spark to gunpowder.

From the time of the government crisis of the autumn of 1899, we, in company with all other foreigners in China, realized that conditions were becoming serious, yet never did we expect or prepare for such a cataclysm as took place when the storm clouds suddenly burst in the early summer of 1900.

The first indication we had of coming danger was when our mail carriers running to and from

Tientsin were stopped and our mails returned. Thus, cut off from the outside world, we had to depend for information solely upon the wild rumors afloat among the Chinese. The country around us became daily more disturbed; day by day we could hear the beating of drums and the cries of the people for rain. The darkness and horror of those days, in the midst of which sickness and death entered our home, can never be forgotten. On June 19 our eldest daughter, Florence, after a week of intense suffering, was released from pain. It was while her life was still hanging in the balance that we received the first communication from the American Consul in Chefoo urging us to flee. This message was quickly followed by another still more urgent.

The question was, Where could we flee? Our usual route was by riverboat two weeks to Tientsin, but this way was blocked, the whole region being infested with Boxers, and Tientsin even then in a state of siege. The only possible route left open to us was southward by cart—fourteen days to Fancheng—then ten or more days by houseboat to Hankow. We faced such a journey at that time of the year with fear and trembling because of the children, the danger from heat and sun being very great. Gladly would we have stayed, but the Chinese Christians urged us to go, saying they could escape more easily were we not there.

We had with us our four remaining children: Paul, nine; Helen, six; Ruth, under three; and baby Wallace, eight months. Their faithful Chinese nurse, though weeping bitterly at parting from her mother of almost eighty, decided to come with us. There were altogether in the party five men, six women, and five children, besides the servants and carters.

Many were the difficulties in the way of getting carts and other necessary things for the journey, but one by one all things needed were provided as we besought the Lord to open the way. There were many indications on that journey that God's purpose was to save us; one of the most striking of these happened just as we were about to leave.

The day previous to our departure a message passed through the city of Chang Te Ho, the messenger riding at breakneck speed. This messenger, we learned later, was en route for the provincial capital with the sealed message from the Empress Dowager commanding the death of all foreigners. We had planned first to take the direct route south, which would, as far as we can now see, have led us through the capital. Almost at the last moment, and quite unaware of the danger on the direct route, we were led to change our plans and take a route farther west, though it made a considerably longer journey.

We left Chang Te, June 28, 1900, at daybreak. At Wei Hwei Fu, the first large city to which we came, an attempt was made to break into our inn, but as we prayed, the mob dispersed and we were left in peace. On July 1 we reached the north bank of the Yellow River, and there for a short time (it was Sunday afternoon), we rested under the trees. Little did we dream that even then many, very many, of our fellow missionaries and personal friends were being put to death by the merciless Boxers. At sunset the ferry which carried us across the river reached the south bank, and here we found several missionaries and a party of engineers waiting for us. These latter were fully armed and had a fair escort. After some difficulty it was decided that we should all keep together, but in reality this party kept by themselves, except that we stayed in the same towns at night. Each day that passed seemed harder than the last, the heat was intense, and the ten or twelve hours of bumping over rough roads in springless carts made even a bed spread on the ground a welcome resting place.

Once, when my husband had jumped off our cart to get fresh water for our head cloths, a crowd gathered round him and became very threatening, raising the cry, "Kill, kill." All the other carts were ahead, and the carter would not wait for Mr. Goforth, as he was afraid. During the few moments that elapsed before my husband was allowed to join us, even the carter turned pale with suspense, and oh, how I prayed!

Except for a few similar passing dangers, nothing special occurred until the evening of July 7, when we reached the small town of Hsintien. We had heard during the day that the whole country ahead of us was in a state of ferment against the Roman Catholics. Scarcely had we reached the inn when the engineers and the missionaries with them, who had become increasingly alarmed at the condition of the country, informed us that they were going on to the large city of Nan Yang Fu that night, but would leave us two soldiers and two of their carts. My husband did not wish them to go, for he felt it would greatly increase our danger.

Shortly after they left us, the mob began to gather outside our inn. The gate was barricaded with carts. For hours stones were thrown against the gate and demand was made for our money. A messenger was at once sent after the engineers' party, asking them to return. All that night was spent in sleepless suspense.

Early in the morning the messenger returned with the reply that they had failed to get help from the Nan Yang Fu official and were obliged to push on. As soon as the carters heard we were thus left helpless, a panic seized them, and it was with great difficulty they could be persuaded to harness their animals. All this time the crowd had been becoming denser, as we could see through the cracks of the gate, and were ominously quiet. Hints had been given us of coming danger, but that was all; none spoke of what all felt—that we were probably going to our death.

Suddenly, without the slightest warning, I was seized with an overwhelming fear of what might be awaiting us. It was not the fear of *after* death, but of probable torture, that took such awful hold of me. I thought, *Can this be the Christian courage I have looked for?* I went by myself and prayed for victory, but no help came. Just then someone called us to a room for prayer before getting into our carts. Scarcely able to walk for trembling and utterly ashamed that others should see my state of panic

—for such it undoubtedly was—I managed to reach a bench beside which my husband stood. He drew from his pocket a little book, *Clarke's Scripture Promises,* and read the verses his eyes first fell upon. They were the following:

The eternal God is thy refuge, and underneath are the everlasting arms: and he shall thrust out the enemy from before thee; and shall say, Destroy them.

The God of Jacob is our refuge.

Thou art my help and my deliverer, make no tarrying, O my God.

I will strengthen thee; yea, I will help thee; yea, I will uphold thee with the right hand of my righteousness. . . . The Lord thy God will hold thy right hand, saying unto thee, Fear not; I will help thee.

If God be for us, who can be against us?

We may boldly say, Thy Lord is my helper, and I will not fear what man shall do unto me.

The effect of these words at such a time was remarkable. All realized that God was speaking to us. Never was there a message more directly given to mortal man from his God than that message to us. From almost the first verse my whole soul seemed flooded with a great peace; all trace of panic vanished; and I felt God's presence was with us. Indeed, His presence was so real it could scarcely have been more so had we seen a visible form.

After prayer we all got on our carts and, one by one, passed out into the densely crowded street. As we approached the city gate we could see that the road was black with crowds awaiting us. I had just remarked to my husband on how well we were getting through the crowds, when our carts passed through the gates. My husband turned pale as he pointed to a group of several hundred men, fully armed, awaiting us. They waited till all the carts had passed through the gate, then hurled down upon us a shower of stones, at the same time rushing forward and maiming or killing some of the animals. My husband jumped down from our cart and cried to them, "Take everything, but don't kill." His only answer was a blow. The confusion that followed was so great it would be impossible to describe the escape of each one in detail. Each one later had his or her own testimony of that mighty and merciful deliverance. But I must give the details of my husband's experience.

One man struck him a blow on the neck with a great sword wielded with two hands. "Somehow" the blunt edge of the sword struck his neck; the blow left a wide mark almost around his neck, but did no further harm. Had the sharp edge struck his neck he would certainly have been beheaded!

His thick helmet was cut almost to pieces, one blow cutting through the leather lining *just over the temple,* but without even scratching the skin!

Again he was felled to the ground, with a fearful sword cut, which entered the bone of the skull behind and almost cleft it in two. As he fell he seemed to hear distinctly a voice saying, "Fear not, they are praying for you." Rising from his blow, he was again struck down by a club. As he was falling almost unconscious to the ground he saw a horse coming at full speed toward him; when be became conscious again he found the horse had tripped and fallen (on level ground) so near that its tail almost touched him. The animal, kicking furiously, had served as a barrier between him and his assailants. While he was dazed and not knowing what to do, a man came up as if to strike, but whispered, "Leave the carts." By that time the onlookers began to rush forward to get the loot, but the attacking party felt the things were theirs, so desisted in their attack upon us in order to secure their booty.

A word as to myself and the children. Several fierce men with swords jumped on my cart. One struck at the baby, but I parried the blow with a pillow, and the little fellow only received a slight scratch on the forehead. Then they dropped their swords and began tearing at our goods at the back of the cart. Heavy boxes were dragged over us, and everything was taken. Just then a dreadful-looking man tried to reach us from the back of the cart with his sword, missing by an inch. I thought he would come to the front and continue his attack, but he did not. I had seen Mr. Goforth sink to the ground covered with blood twice, and had given him up for dead. Just then Paul, who had been in the last cart, jumped in, wild with delight at what he seemed to think was great fun, for he had run through the thick of the fight, dodging sword thrusts from all sides, and had succeeded in reaching me without a scratch. A moment later my husband came to the edge of the cart scarcely able to stand, saying, "Get down quickly; we must not delay in getting away." As I was getting down one man snatched away my hat, another my shoes; but we were allowed to go.

Ruth was nowhere to be seen, and we hoped she was with the missionaries who had charge of her at the time of attack. I saw that my husband's strength was failing fast for he could scarcely talk, and as men began to follow I urged him forward with the baby and the other two children, and turning faced the men, begging them to have mercy on my children, for they had begun to stone us. Some of us were black for days from the blows received then. They stopped and listened, then the leader said, "We've killed her husband, let her go." With this they ran back to the carts.

I knew Mr. Goforth could not go far. We could see a small village not far distant, and to this we hastened, praying as we went that the Lord would open the hearts of the people to receive us. Here again Paul seemed to feel no fear, but said, "Mother, what does this put you in mind of? It puts me in mind of the Henty books!"

As we neared the village, men came out to drive us away, but I begged them to help us. By this time Mr. Goforth had sunk to the ground. Putting the baby in an old woman's arms, I knelt down beside my husband. The children were crying bitterly. Mr. Goforth looked as if he were dying. The women standing round us were weeping now. This was too much for the men, who came forward saying, "We will save you." One ran and got some stuff to put in the wounds, assuring us it would stop the flow of blood, and it did. This man helped me to bandage up the wounds with bandages made from garments taken from myself and the children. They helped my husband, and we followed them into a little hut, where they laid him on a straw bed and locked us in. Hot water for bathing our bruises, food, and drink were handed us through a small window, and we could hear them planning how they would save us. We told them how anxious we were to hear of our friends and little Ruth, so they sent a man to inquire.

We found that these people—the whole village— were Muslims and had taken no part in the attack. We felt that God had wonderfully directed our steps to that village.

All that day Mr. Goforth lay still, but looked at times so very white that I feared the worst. Never for one moment, I believe, during that day did I cease to pray for his life. And when one of our party arrived about four o'clock looking for us, my husband at once got up as if perfectly well, insisting on walking to the cart. To me, knowing how he had looked that day, it seemed only a miracle. His only answer to my protest was, "Only pray; the Lord will give me strength, as long as He has work for me to do."

As we were leaving, the kind friends of the village gathered round insisting on my taking some old clothes to put around the children, who were almost naked, saying, "It will be chilly at night."

As we went forward to join the others, they told us how one by one all had escaped. The doctor was the only one besides my husband seriously injured, the poor fellow having had his kneecap severed and the tendons of his right wrist badly cut, besides many other wounds.

All that day our friends had been waiting by the roadside, unable to proceed without carts, owing to the doctor's condition. They had joined in one petition, that God would move the carters to come. Those who know China and heathen carters will readily acknowledge that it was nothing short of a miracle—the miracle of answered prayer—that made these heathen carters came, after all they had already gone through. For come they did, five of them, all that were needed, now that our luggage was gone. We learned too that our faithful Chinese nurse, who had charge of Ruth, had saved the child and taken many cruel blows. till greed for loot drew the men off.

We soon joined the rest of the party, and by six o'clock that evening, we reached the large city of Nang Yang Fu. The city wall was black with people, and as we entered the gate the wild crowds crushed against our carts. Sometimes the animals staggered, and it seemed as if nothing could save the carts from being overturned. Every moment or two a brick or stone would be hurled against the carts, and that cry, "Kill, kill," which can never be forgotten when once heard, was shouted by perhaps hundreds of voices. Yet the Lord brought us through, and "no weapon prospered."

When we reached the inn a wild mob of over a thousand men filled the inn yard; and as we alighted from the cart these men literally drove us before them into one room, which in a few moments was packed to suffocation. For probably an hour the crowd kept crushing us into one corner; then those outside became impatient at not being able to get in, and demanded that we be brought out. We managed to keep some of the ladies from going out; but the rest of us—men, women, and children—stood facing that seething multitude until relief came in the darkness. Why did they not kill us then? Why, indeed? None but an Almighty God kept that crowd back.

As soon as we had reached the city a servant was sent to the official demanding protection. It was dark when this man returned, in a state of great agitation; his story was that as he was waiting for an answer from the official he overheard a conversation between two soldiers and gathered from what they said that the official had sent a party of fifty soldiers along the road that we would have to take, with the order that every one of us must be put to death. The official was afraid to have us killed in the city lest he should afterward be blamed; but by this plan he could say brigands had done the deed. So sure was this servant that we were all to be massacred that he would remain with us no longer but returned that night to Honan with the report that we were all killed.

A consultation was held, and the question was, Should we stay in the city and again demand protection, or should we go on and trust God to open our way? The latter course was decided upon. But for a long time the carters utterly refused to go farther with us. Again prayer opened up our way, and by two o'clock in the morning all were ready to start.

The official had sent a few foot-soldiers to guide us to *the right road!* (to the waylaying party). The night was very dark, and as we were passing through the gate of the city we noticed what seemed to be signal lights put out and drawn in. We all felt these to be signals to the waylaying party ahead. A short distance from the city, probably about one hundred yards, our carts suddenly stopped. Some-one ran up and whispered to my husband, "Paul and another man are missing." Search was made for them without success.

A veil must be drawn over those terrible hours of suspense; my faith seemed to fail me, and I could only cry in my agony, "If Paul is gone, can I ever trust God again?" Then I remembered how marvelously God had given me back my dear husband's life, and I just committed Paul into His hands and waited to see what He would do.

When all hope was given up of finding the missing ones, a cart was left behind with a trusted servant, and we went on. Then we saw God's wonderful plan for us. While we were waiting the soldiers had fallen asleep in the carts, and were not aware that the carters were taking a side road until we had gotten miles from the city and beyond the reach of our would-be murderers! The soldiers were infuriated at this discovery; but after some threatening they left us and returned to the city. Thus again we saw that God was indeed unto us a "God of deliverances."

Again and again that day we were surrounded by mobs. Many times I held up the poor, dirty clothes which the Muslims had given us, and the story of how these had been given quieted the people perhaps more than anything. Once the cry was raised to drag our children's nurse out of the cart; but as we cried to God for her the people let us alone, and we passed on. At another time a man snatched the remains of Mr. Goforth's helmet from us, and tore it to pieces. I had hoped to keep it as a trophy should we ever get out safely.

We were at this time in a pitiable condition. Most of the men had head or arms bandaged; the doctor was unable to raise his head. What we suffered in those carts with nothing but the boards under us cannot be told. Nine persons were packed in our cart, which under ordinary circumstances would have held four or five. At noon we reached a large city, where the animals had to rest and feed. Then again we saw an evidence of the Lord's lovingkindness over us.

Just as we were getting down from our carts the crowd became very threatening, and it looked now as if our hour had indeed come; but at this critical juncture two well-dressed young men of official class came through the crowd, greeting my husband in great surprise. They had been received by him in our home at Chang Te Ho. A few words of explanation were spoken, then they turned quickly to the crowd and told them who we were and of the work at Chang Te Ho. The attitude of the people changed instantly, and they made way for us, giving us good rooms, and food was brought which was greatly needed.

That noon, as one after another came up to express their sympathy at Paul's loss, I could say nothing—I was waiting to see what God would do. When Mr. Goforth told the young officials about Paul and the other man, they were greatly concerned and promised to send men at once to search for them. These friends in need sent with us a man of the district to guide and help us and also wrote an urgent letter to the official of the city to give us an escort and help us in every way he could.

About four o'clock that afternoon a man came running after us with the joyful news that Paul and our friend were safe, and would reach us that night. As I heard this news my unbelief and faithlessness in the hour of testing came over me with overwhelming force, and I could only bow my head and weep. Oh, the goodness and mercy of God! Never had the love of God seemed so wonderful as in that hour.

> Could we with ink the ocean fill,
>   Were the whole sky of parchment made,
> Were every blade of grass a quill,
>   And every man a scribe by trade;
> To write the love of God above
>   Would drain that ocean dry,

> Nor could the scroll contain the whole
> Though stretched from sky to sky.

That night we reached our destination about nine o'clock, having traveled seventeen hours over those roads, with but a short break at noon. It was marvelous how Mr. Goforth was sustained, for he was obliged to start at once for the official's residence with the note I have already referred to. On the way through the street the mob about succeeded several times in getting him down under their feet; but God was with him, and he reached the yamen in safety, being courteously received by the official, who promised us protection and sent him back to the inn under escort.

When Paul and the other man arrived that night, they tried in vain to wake me, but nature had to have her way. I knew nothing till I wakened with a start at about 2 A.M. Jumping up, I started to look for Paul, and never can I forget the scene! The whole party was lying on the bare earthen floor, practically without bedding or mattresses.

A word concerning the experiences of our friend and Paul. The two had gotten down from their cart and were walking behind. In some way they missed the road in the dark, and became separated from us. During that day they were repeatedly in the gravest danger.

On one occasion, when surrounded by a violent mob, and one man had raised a club above Paul's head to strike him down, this friend felt impelled by some unseen power to shout out, "We are not

Roman Catholics, but Protestants." At this the man lowered his club, exclaiming, "Why, these are not the bad foreign devils, but the good foreign devils, like those missionaries at Chow Chia K'eo" (China Inland Mission). At this same place the hearts of the people seemed turned toward them in a wonderful way. One man gave Paul one hundred *cash* (five cents) to buy some food; another man carried the lad on his back for miles to give his feet a rest, they were so sore. This same man, when he could carry Paul no longer, ran ahead to try to find us. When they reached the inn where we had been so helped by the two Chinese gentlemen, they found that these friends had food prepared and a barrow waiting, also a guide ready to lead them to us!

Less than an hour from the time I awakened we were on the road again. The official was true to his promise, and a large mounted escort accompanied us. That day we were on the road twenty hours, reaching Fan Cheng at midnight. Here we found the engineers' party waiting for us with boats hired, but we were obliged to remain twenty-four hours in the most loathsome inn in which we ever had the misfortune to be in China. It was an unspeakable relief to get into the houseboats, even though we only had bare boards to lie on, and the boat people's food to eat.

We were ten days going downstream to Hankow. One after the other became ill. When still a day from Hankow, a steam tug met us with provisions. Our children cried at the sight of bread and milk! We were not allowed to stop long enough at Hankow, as we had hoped, to get clothes and other necessities, but were obliged to hasten on by the first steamer, which left the following morning. I was obliged to borrow garments for myself and the children from our fellow passengers.

At Shanghai the streets were being paraded, and every preparation was being made for an attack. We learned with deep sorrow of the death of many dear friends at the hands of the Boxers. Ordered home by the first steamer, without anything left to us but the old clothes we had on at the time of the attack, how could we get ready in such a short time for the long home voyage? There was no lack of money, for our Board had cabled all we needed. The question that faced us was how could I get clothes made for six of us in such a short time, with Chinese tailors too busy to help, no machine to be had, and no ready-made clothes to be bought except for Mr. Goforth and Paul?

Again I found that man's extremity was but God's opportunity. He was true to His promise "God shall supply all your need." Even as I knelt in an agony of prayer, beseeching God's help, and asking definitely that someone should be sent to me to help with the sewing, two ladies were at the door asking for me! These were perfect strangers, but had seen our names among the recent refugees, and God had moved them to come and offer their assistance! They worked for me night and day until we had to get on board the steamer. Never shall I forget their Christian fellowship and practical help at that time.

But in the rush to get the other children ready, baby Wallace's clothes were neglected. There was nothing for it but to take materials and make things for him on the voyage. In this connection came a most wonderful and precious evidence of God's power to answer prayer. For the first few days of the journey I worked early and late trying to make something for the little one, who had scarcely anything to wear; but as we were nearing Yokohama I realized I had almost reached the end of my strength. My needle refused to work; try as I would I could not even see where to put the needle.

Folding up my work I went down to the stateroom, and, kneeling down, I spread the work before the Lord. Too far gone to agonize in prayer, I could only quietly, almost mutely, just tell Him how the poor child had no clothes. Rising with a great sense of the burden having been lifted, I put the work away, locking it in a trunk, then went up on deck and lay down almost insensible from exhaustion. How long a time passed I do not know, but it could not have been more than half an hour when someone came and touched me, saying, "We have dropped anchor in Yokohama Bay, and a large bundle has been thrown up on deck from the lighter for you."

"For me!" I cried. "Surely not, I know no one in Japan." Then I thought, *It is the answer come!*

Going down I found a letter from Mrs. O. E., of the China Inland Mission. She said that her little son, the same age as baby Wallace, had died four months before, and the Lord had pressed her to send his complete oufit to me for my child! Opening the parcel, I found not only everything the child could possibly need for a year or more, but much else. Had someone stood beside that dear sister and told her what I most needed, she could not have done differently. Yes, surely Someone did direct her loving hands, and Someone just used her as one of His channels; for she lived near to Him and was an open channel.

Three days later my own collapse came; but praise His great name. He was with me in the darkness and brought me through.

6

Proving God's Faithfulness
(1902-1908)

The safest place . . . is the path of duty.

One of the results of our gracious and merciful deliverance from the hands of the Boxers was an increased desire to make our lives tell in the service of God—to spend and be spent for Him. Our heavenly Father saw this and just took us at our word and led us out into the path which meant absolute surrender as I had never known it before.

It is so true that "God will be no man's debtor." When He asks for and receives our all, He gives in return that which is above price—His own presence. The price is not great when compared with what He gives in return; it is our blindness and our unwillingness to yield that make it seem great.

The following story has been asked for many times. Believing that it has a lesson for others, I give it, though to do so means lifting the veil from a very sacred part of my life.

After the Boxer experience, my husband returned to China in 1901; and, with my children, I left for China in the summer of 1902, leaving the two eldest children at the Chefoo schools, en route to Honan. Mr. Goforth met me at Tientsin, and together we traveled by riverboat inland a journey of about twenty-four days. During those long, quiet days on the riverboat, my husband unfolded to me a carefully thought-out plan for future mission work.

He reminded me that six missionaries, from a mission station which had been destroyed by the Boxers, were now permanently stationed at Changte; and that the main station, now fully equipped, no longer needed us as before. He felt that the time had come when we should give ourselves to the evangelization of the great regions north and northeast of Changte, regions which up to that time had been scarcely touched by the Gospel, because of lack of workers. His plan was that we—husband and wife, with our children—should go and live and work among the people.

To make this possible a native compound would be rented in the center, where we would stay a month for our first visit, leaving behind an evangelist to carry on the work; and we would revisit this and other places so opened as many times as possible in the year.

What this proposition meant to me can scarcely be understood by those unfamiliar with China and Chinese life. Smallpox, diphtheria, scarlet fever and other contagious diseases are chronic epidemics; and China, outside the parts ruled by foreigners, is absolutely devoid of sanitation.

Four of our children had died. To take the three little ones, then with me, into such conditions and danger seemed literally like stepping with them over a precipice in the dark and expecting to be kept. But, on the other hand, I had the language and experience for just such work, the need was truly appalling, and there was no other woman to do it. In my innermost soul I knew the call had come from God, but I would not pay the price. My one plea in refusing to enter that life was the risk to the children.

Again and again my husband urged that "the safest place" for myself and the children "was the path of duty"; that I could not keep them in our comfortable home at Changte, but "God could keep them anywhere." Still I refused. Just before reaching our station he begged me to reconsider my decision. When I gave a final refusal, his only answer was, "I fear for the children."

The very day after reaching home our dear Wallace was taken ill. For weeks we fought for his life; at last the crisis passed and he began to recover. Then my husband started off alone on his first trip! He had been gone only a day or two when our precious baby Constance, a year old, was taken down with the same disease that Wallace had. From the first there seemed little or no hope. The doctors, a nurse, and all the little mission circle joined in the fight for her life. Her father was sent for but arrived just as she was losing consciousness. A few hours later, when we were kneeling round her bedside waiting for the end, my eyes seemed suddenly opened to what I had been doing: *I had dared to fight against Almighty God.*

In the moments that followed God revealed Himself to me in such love and majesty and glory that I gave myself to Him with unspeakable joy. Then I knew that I had been making an awful mistake and that I could indeed safely trust my children to Him wherever He might lead. One thing only seemed plain, that I must follow where God should lead. I saw at last that God must come first. Before the precious body was laid away, preparations for our first trip were begun.

Was God faithful to the vision He had given me? Or did He allow the children to suffer in the years that followed, when months each year were spent with them right out among the people? As I write this, eighteen years have passed since we started on that first trip, and none of our children has died. Never had we as little sickness as during that life. Never had we so much evidence of God's favor and blessing in a hundred ways—as may be gathered from the definite testimonies which follow.

Without one exception, every place in which we stayed for a month, and opened as my husband had planned, became in time a growing church.

And I found, to my surprise, that I was able to give more time to the children, that I was able to guard them better when on those trips than when in the Changte station. For the mission compound was large, and often the children were out of my sight for hours at a time; whereas the outside native compounds we lived in were so small the children were always within sight and reach. Even when groups of women were listening to the Gospel, I was able to direct the children's lessons. As I look back on that time, my heart is filled with overflowing gratitude to God for the wonderful grace and strength He gave for that life.

My great regret is that I did not keep a record of answers to prayer. I find it most difficult to record just what "asking and getting things from God" meant at that time, but it now seems to me to have been the very foundation of the whole life. The instances of answers to prayer, here recorded, are simply the ones connected with that life which stand out most clearly in my memory of those years.

The first answer came the morning after our dear Constance died, and was the one that had the greatest, most far-reaching effect on the new life and its work.

As I thought of facing the crowds of heathen women day by day, and what it would mean to carry on aggressive evangelism outside, there was one need I felt must be met—that of a Bible woman. As I prayed for direction, a Mrs. Wang Hsieh-sheng came to mind as the one I should ask.

But when I laid my request before her, that she come with me, she burst into tears, saying: "I dare not. I have only one child left, and it would risk her life too much."

Seeing how she felt, I did not urge her but told her to go and pray about it for a day, and bring me her answer after the funeral that night. When she came that evening her face was shining through tears, as she said, "Oh my shepherd mother, I will go. If you are willing to risk your children for the sake of my sisters, how much more should I!"

Eighteen years have passed since that day. I would need to write a volume to record all that Mrs. Wang meant to me, yes, and to the work in those years. As the years passed she became my beloved companion, sharing in all the responsibilities and hardships of that life, and also in its joys. I realized more and more that she was indeed a God-given co-worker. Though circumstances have led me away from that life, she still remains and works for her sisters in the Changte church.

One of the hardest words a missionary can get from his home board is the word *retrench*. My husband and I were on one of our evangelistic tours north of Changte. Every door seemed wide open before us, and the time ripe for an especially aggressive campaign of evangelism. But, just as we were planning for this, word reached us from our station treasurer of a message received from the home board that funds were low, and retrenchment must be carried out along all lines.

To us this meant dismissing helpers, and a general curtailing of our work. We faced the question squarely. Our own tithe had been long overdrawn. How then could we support the men we had, and go on with the work which was opening so gloriously before us after years of hard pioneer preparation?

But we decided to go on as we had planned, and to trust God for the necessary funds; believing that, though for the time being the home church had disappointed us, God would not fail us.

The following Friday a home mail reached us, in which was a letter from a lady in New Zealand. The writer said she had read a letter of ours in *The Life of Faith*, and wished to support an evangelist under us. This relieved us of the support of one man, but there were many other needs as yet unmet.

The following Monday, when our next mail was forwarded to us, a letter came from a lady in Australia, enclosing a draft ample to meet every special need in the work for a year to come. She stated very plainly that she did not wish the money put into the general funds of the mission, but to be used by ourselves in any way we thought best. Indeed, had she known the special circumstances in which the letter would find us, she could scarcely have written more exactly to fit our case.

Again, a year after this experience of God's faithfulness to meet all our needs, we began to feel the need of special funds for the work. My husband, as usual, seemed quite sure that we should keep on as we had been doing, and that the money needed would be sent. In spite of all the blessed lessons of the past, my faith seemed to fail me; and I spoke decidedly against using our salary, when we needed it all for ourselves and our children's education. We were traveling homeward by cart at the time and the matter was dropped; though I felt my husband was hurt by my lack of faith.

When we reached home that evening, a letter from a lady in Canada was awaiting my husband. He read it first; and I cannot forget the look on his face as he handed it to me, with the words "I told you so."

As near as I can recall it the letter said: "My mother and I are strangers to you, never having seen or heard either you or your wife. But my mother, who is an invalid, has for some time been restless because of a conviction that has come over her that she should send you some money. So to quiet my mother I am sending you fifty dollars."

As I read the letter, I certainly did feel ashamed of my lack of faith. In writing our acknowledgment, I told how wonderfully opportune the gift had been. A couple of months or so later came a reply, telling us that the invalid mother passed away soon after my letter reached them and that the story of how God had used her faith had blessed and helped her during the closing days of her life.

On one occasion, when we were traveling from Wuanhsien to Pengcheng, we reached the town of Hotsun late in the afternoon, expecting to stay overnight. But on our arrival we found that the Christian whom we had sent to arrange for our accommodation had failed to get us a place, everyone absolutely refusing to take us in. While the animals were feeding, and we were trying to eat our dinner of Chinese dough-strings in the midst of a curious crowd, my husband told the Christian to go out again and look for a place while we prayed.

We dared not close our eyes, lest the superstitious crowd crushing against us on all sides would take fright, thinking we were mesmerizing them. So we just lifted up our hearts silently to our Father; and before many minutes had passed, indeed before we had finished our meal, the Christian returned greatly rejoiced, saying, "A wealthy man has offered you a fine empty place which has just been fixed over. And you can have it as long as you like, free of rent."

For three days we preached in that place—morning, noon, and night—to great crowds; and a work was begun which has gone on ever since.

There were times when my faith was severely tested, and I fear too often I did not stand the test; but, oh, how patient God is with us in our human weakness! "Like as a father pitieth . . . so the Lord pitieth." The Chinese have often said to me, "Your children seem made for this life." But I know it was God's great goodness. He knew how hard the life was, and how difficult it would have been for me to continue that work had the children been peevish or hard to manage. Time and time again we had to get the little ones up before daybreak to start on a cart journey, but I do not remember that they ever even cried. They would just wake up enough to get dressed and ask sleepily, "Are we going again, Mamma?" and then go off to sleep as soon as we were settled in our carts.

On one occasion, arriving at a certain town, we found the place in which we were to stay unfit for the children. It was simply horrible. On either side of us, almost reaching to our door, were two great pigsties—Chinese pigsties! In front of the door were eight or ten great vessels, filled with fermenting stuff which had been there all summer, and which added to the other varied and oppressive odors. I greatly feared for the children, and wanted to leave at once, but my husband seemed calmly certain of the Lord's power to keep them from all harm.

On the second evening the youngest child became feverish. Mr. Goforth was holding a meeting with the men. I was almost overwhelmed with fear lest the child had diphtheria. Kneeling down beside him, I cried to the Lord as only a mother under like circumstances could pray. At last, tired out, I fell asleep on my knees. Awakened by the entrance of my husband, I felt the child's head again and it seemed cooler, and the child quieter. The following day he was quite well. Is it much wonder I can say I know God answers prayer?

Returning from our summer holiday September 1, 1912, we hoped to find a place rented at a certain large center where we had planned to begin work; but to our disappointment learned that the evangelists had secured premises in a small market village, where there was just one Christian. There was nothing to do but to go there, though it seemed almost useless, for it was the busiest season for those farming people.

On our way to this place we prayed much that

the Lord would prepare the people, and open their hearts to the Gospel. We had not been there many days when we became convinced that we had been led there, and that the Lord was opening the hearts of the people in a most unusual way. Crowds of men and women heard the preaching every day. Our evening gospel meetings, with organ and hymn scroll, were crowded out on the street.

Everywhere we met with the utmost friendliness, and before our month's visit was ended, we had the joy of seeing some of the leading people in the village and district come out boldly for Christ. One was the chief doctor; another was the head man in the market. In the store, through which we women had to pass to get to the evening meeting, there were three men and a young lad of fifteen; all of these were brought to Christ. The men were opium users, gamblers, men of evil lives. Two of them are now preachers of the Gospel, and one is the leading man in the little growing church there.

Had I time and space I could go on multiplying cases where the same results have followed when the cross of Christ has been the pivot of all Christian teaching, and prayer has been the source of power.

On one of the early visits to the city of Linchang, a woman came with a little child whose foot was terribly burned. The whole foot was badly swollen, the inflammation reaching some distance up the leg. The child was feverish and seemed in a serious condition. It happened that on that trip I had forgotten to bring the simple remedies which I was accustomed to take out with me, so the woman was told nothing could be done. But she begged so piteously that I could not turn away; and lifting up my heart in prayer I asked the Lord to guide me, if there was anything I could do.

Even while I prayed the thought of a bread poultice came to mind. This remedy seemed almost absurd. I had never heard of such a thing being used before under like circumstances, but I resolved to try it. Twice a day the foot was cleansed and put in the poultice, and it was really wonderful to see how it healed. We were there ten days, and when we left the foot was almost completely well. The mother, father, the child herself, and indeed the whole family, became Christians. On a later visit I examined the foot and found not even the sign of a scar remaining.

I told this incident to a medical doctor, and he said, "Why, there is no miracle in *that!* It was just up-to-date hygiene—giving nature a chance by cleanliness!"

I replied, "Doctor, to me the miracle lay, not in the poultice, but in God's telling me what to use; and now it is to me all the more a miracle of prayer, since you say it was up-to-date hygienic treatment."

At the same place, some years later, we were conducting special tent meetings for Christians in the daytime and for the unsaved at night. Just after our meetings began the weather turned bitterly cold, with wind and sleety rain. The tent was like a drafty icehouse. My husband caught a severe cold, which became worse each day. He had fever and severe pains in head and chest but would not give up his meetings. One noon he came from the meeting looking very ill and lay down to rest till the afternoon meeting.

I determined to take the Christians into my confidence, and tell them of my anxiety for my husband. So, some time before the afternoon meeting I slipped out and called them into the tent, telling them of my husband's condition and asking them to pray for him. Oh, what a wave of earnest, heart-overflow of prayer went up without a moment's pause! The tears came to my eyes as I thought, *Surely God will answer such prayers!*

Then, fearing my husband might arrive, I gave out a hymn. A few moments later he walked into the tent in his brisk way, looking quite well. At the close of the meeting he told me that shortly after he heard me go out, the pain in his head and chest ceased, the fever seemed to leave him, and when he started for the tent he felt quite well. The symptoms did not return.

When on a visit to a certain outstation, after being there two whole days, scarcely any women had come to see us. We were so circumstanced that I could not leave the children. The third day I became so burdened in prayer that I could only shut myself up in an empty room and cry to the Lord to send women to us, as He knew I could not leave the children. From that day we always had plenty of visitors to keep us busy, either Christian women studying or unsaved women listening to the Gospel.

At Tzuchow, the first place we opened together, the people seemed much set against us. After the first period of curiosity was over, no one came to hear the Gospel. As we had a nice place for the children to play in with their faithful nurse—the one who saved Ruth's life in 1900—Mrs. Wang and I determined to go out each afternoon and try to reach the heathen women with the Gospel. Before going out we always prayed the Lord to open a door to us for preaching. And as I now recall that time, never once did we return home without being invited into some home to preach, or at least being asked to sit on a doorstep and tell of the Saviour from sin.

One of the most outstanding evidences of God's favor and blessing was seen, at this time, in the way He provided my husband with native helpers. To carry on the plan of work we had adopted required a good force of trusty evangelists. Time and again we looked to the Lord for men and women to help us, and the answer always came.

As my husband always seemed to have plenty of men to help him, he was frequently asked for evangelists by his fellow missionaries of both our own and other missions. I was at first opposed to his giving away his best men, but he would answer, "The Lord has been good to me; should I be less generous with my brethren?" And it certainly was remarkable how, whenever he gave a really valuable evangelist, another man, even better, was raised up shortly after. The secret of his getting men may be seen best through words of his own, taken from a letter to a friend in Canada about the time of which I am now writing:

"We came to this little market town in September of last year. My wife had two women workers. I had Mr. Tung, the old evangelist, and a young high school graduate without experience, and the only Christian man in the district, very ignorant but with this to recommend him, that he was converted or quickened by the Holy Spirit in the Changte revival, and was intensely in earnest. We were here only about twenty days when dozens began to inquire, among whom were robbers, opium sots, and gamblers. The work went on all day and well on till midnight. We were all tiring out. We had not enough workers. It was like a very heavy burden that forced me to my knees. I told the Lord that He was the Lord of the harvest, and that He must send more harvesters. There was a time of intense looking to God, almost amounting to agony, and then the burden lifted, and I knew that God had answered. I told my wife that I was sure that God was going to send me workers.

"Now what is the result? Since then He has sent me two Chinese B.A.s, both excellent speakers. He moved an excellent elder to give up his business, and he has been appointed an evangelist. At this center a scholar, who was an opium user and gambler, got converted last year. His progress has been most remarkable, and it looks as if he is going to make one of the front-rank preachers. Also two brothers here, who were among the first converts last year, help to preach; their father—also a convert of last year—providing their food."

Another gracious evidence of God's overruling providence was seen in the way we, especially the children, were kept from contracting diseases. The Chinese carry their children about everywhere in their arms, even when sick with all sorts of contagious diseases.

I give the following instance to show how impossible it was to know when one would run into danger. Going to a certain village for a day's preaching, I took with me little Mary, then three years of age. We were waited on by a Christian woman who was most kind and attentive, bringing water and food for both Mary and myself. Being much taken up with preaching to the woman, it did not occur to me to ask why she kept her baby's face covered, for the child was always in her arms. Just as we were leaving I asked her; then she uncovered the baby's face, and to my horror I found that the child was suffering from smallpox! For weeks I watched Mary's temperature, but nothing developed.

Through repeated instances of this kind I came to see that Mr. Goforth was right when he said, "The safest place for yourself and the children is in the path of duty."

As I recall those years of touring life with our children, words fail me to tell of all the Lord's goodness to them and to me. Though there were many hard, hard places, these were but opportunities for special grace and help. Many times, when discouraged almost to the point of never going out again with the children, there would come evidence that the Lord was using our family life, lived among the people, to win them to Christ. Then I would take new courage and go again. It is so true that

> We may trust Him fully
>   All for us to do;
> Those who trust Him wholly
>   Find Him wholly true.

7

The Story of One Furlough (1908-1910)

Call upon me in the day of trouble: I will deliver thee, and thou shalt glorify me. PSALM 50:15

In the summer of 1908, I was obliged to return to Canada with five of our children, leaving my husband in China for the revival work.

Reaching Toronto, I learned that my eldest son was at death's door from repeated attacks of rheumatic fever. He was then almost a day's journey away. On my way there, as I recalled the times in which he had been given back to us from the very gates of death, my faith was strengthened to believe for his recovery again. But, as I prayed, it became very clear that the answer to my petition depended on myself; in other words, that I must yield myself and my will to God.

I had been planning to take no meetings during that furlough, but to devote myself wholly to my children. I confessed the sin of planning my own life and definitely covenanted with the Lord that if He would raise my son for His service, I would take meetings, or do anything, as He opened the way for the care of the children.

There were six difficult doors, however, that would have to be opened—not one, but all—before I could possibly go out and speak for Christ and China, as God seemed to be asking. First, the Lord would need to restore my son to complete health, as I could never feel justified in leaving a sick child. Second, He would need to restore my own health, for I had been ordered to the hospital for an operation. Third, He would need to keep all the other children well. Fourth, a servant must be sent to take care of the house—though my income was so small that a servant seemed out of the question, and only the strictest economy was making both ends meet. Fifth, a Christian lady would need to be willing to take care of the children, and act as my housekeeper in my absence from home. Sixth, sufficient money would need to be sent to meet the extra expenses incurred by my leaving home.

Yet, as I laid these difficulties before the Lord, I received the definite assurance that He would open the way.

My son was brought back to Toronto on a stretcher, the doctor not allowing him to raise his head; but on arrival he would not obey orders, declaring that he was so well he could not and would not remain still. Fearing the consequences of his disobeying orders, I telephoned for the doctor to come at once. On his arrival he gave the lad a thorough examination, and then said, "Well, I cannot make him out; all I can say is, let him do as he pleases."

Within a month the boy was going back to his high school, apparently quite well. Some months later he applied for a position as forester under the government. He had to pass through the hands of the official doctor. My son told him of his recent illness, and of what the doctor had said concerning his heart; but this physician replied, "In spite of all you have told me I can discover nothing whatever the matter with you, and I will therefore give you a clear bill of health."

As for myself, I did not go to the hospital; for all the symptoms that had seemed to require it left me, and I became perfectly well. A servant was sent to me who did her work sympathetically, as helping me to do the Lord's work. A married niece, living near, offered to stay in the home whenever I needed to be absent.

And so there remained but one condition unfulfilled—the money. But I believed this would come as I went forward; and it did. Each month that followed, as I made up my accounts, I found that my receipts exceeded my expenditures sufficiently to enable me to spend money for work in China, and to purchase things which I needed in China, including an organ. All these accounts were laid before our beloved mission board secretary, who approved them.

Under these circumstances I dared not refuse invitations to speak. Yet so weak was my faith that for months I never left home for a few days without dreading lest something should happen to the children during my absence. I even accepted meetings with the proviso that if the children needed me I must fail to keep my appointment. But as the days and weeks and months passed, and all went well, I learned to trust.

"Be still; be strong today."
   But, Lord, tomorrow?
What of tomorrow, Lord?
Shall there be rest from toil,
   Be truce from sorrow?
"Did I not die for thee?
Do I not live for thee?
   Leave Me tomorrow."

In giving the following I wish to make clear that, had I been living a life of ease or self-indulgence, I could not have been justified in expecting God to undertake for me in such matters as are here recorded. It must be remembered that I had stepped out into a life which meant *trusting for everything*.

Before leaving China for Canada my husband had said to me, "Do not limit the children's apples; give them all they want." But when I began housekeeping I found this was not very easy to do. Apples were expensive, and the appetites of my six children for them seemed insatiable. However, I began by buying a few small baskets; and then I did not need to buy more, for apples came in a most wonderful way. First in baskets; then, as the season advanced, in barrels. These came from many different sources;

and in some cases long distances, express paid to the door. On one occasion a barrel of large, hard Greenings came just as we had finished the last barrel. The children complained that they were too hard to eat, and begged me to buy them some Snows —very expensive, but delicious apples for eating. I had only purchased one small basket of Snows when a large supply, almost a barrelful, came from a distant friend.

I feel that the Lord saw that I had given up all for Him, so just showed how He could provide, thus evidencing His love and care for my dear children. We had set up housekeeping at the end of the fruit season, and so I had not been able to do canning for winter use. That winter, again and again, gifts of canned fruit came, sometimes from unknown sources. Altogether seventy jars of the finest fruit were sent to us. I will give the details of just one of these gifts.

Shortly before leaving home for ten days, the servant informed me that the canned fruit was finished. Accordingly I went down and ordered enough dried fruit to last till I should return. On reaching home I was greeted at the door by a rush from the children, all trying at once to tell me that a lovely valentine had just arrived. Leading me back to the kitchen, they showed me the table covered with twenty jars of the most delicious-looking fruit, and a large can of maple syrup. On a card accompanying the gift was written: "A valentine for our dear 'substitute in China,' from her sisters in Renfrew."

Early in the winter it became evident that a telephone was a necessity, with my numerous calls and engagements. I hesitated about going into this expense, not being quite sure that it was right to use in that way the money given me. At last, I prayed that the Lord would show me His will in the matter by sending me half the amount needed for the telephone within a certain time, if it was right for me to get it. Before the time expired the money had come; so I got the telephone.

As the cold weather set in I began to suffer on the long drives in the country to appointments, and was soon longing for a fur coat. I consulted our mission secretary as to whether, if sufficient money were given me, I could put it into a fur coat. The answer was a decided yes. There was no doubt that the coat was a necessity in the Lord's work. So I began to pray the Lord to send the money quickly, for the cold was severe. In less than two weeks I received the money needed and, of course, got the coat.

The ladies of the Winnipeg Presbyterial had arranged a series of meetings for me in Winnipeg, Brandon, and other places in that vicinity, about ten in all. The collections from the meetings were to defray my traveling expenses, which would amount to more than one hundred dollars. On my way by train from Toronto to Winnipeg I caught a severe cold, which settled in my throat and chest. I did not want the women to be disappointed, and also put to all the expense, if I failed them. Just before reaching Winnipeg I was enabled to commit myself definitely into the Lord's hands for strength and voice for the meetings. The days that followed can never be forgotten, for the bodily weakness, fever, and throat trouble were removed only while I was giving my addresses. In each case, though so hoarse before and after speaking as to be scarcely able to make myself heard above a whisper, my voice cleared for the address.

For example, while at Dr. and Mrs. C. W. Gordon's home the Sunday I was to speak in Winnipeg, I was advertised to speak that night in Dr. Gordon's church. At the supper table I asked Dr. Gordon if he would be ready to speak should I fail. Just before my time came to speak I slipped up on to the platform behind Dr. Gordon, who was praying; and oh, how I cried to the Lord for help and courage! For the church was packed, and even the Sunday school room partitions were opened to accommodate the crowd. My throat was as if in a vise, and I felt weak and ill. But, as Dr. Gordon introduced me, I stepped forward possessed by a feeling of wonderful calm and absolute confidence. It seemed I could just *feel* One like unto the Son of man beside me, and never had I felt so completely and only a channel. For more than an hour I spoke so that everyone heard distinctly; but when I sat down my throat tightened as before. Dr. Gordon told me later that he had a man sit in the most difficult place in which to hear, and that he had heard every word.

So it was till the end of my appointments. On the homeward journey I asked the Lord either to heal my throat, or to provide a way for me to get a needed rest from speaking, for I had many appointments awaiting me in Ontario. A few days after reaching home four of my children were taken down with measles. During the weeks I was in quarantine with them my throat received the rest it needed, and became quite restored.

One day the following early summer, in looking over the children's clothes, I found there was so much to be done I was fairly overwhelmed. I saw it was quite impossible to do the necessary sewing and keep my appointments too. The question that weighed heavily was, "Should I cancel the meetings for which I had given my word?" My husband urged me to buy ready-made clothes, but I knew how expensive they would be and could not bring myself to do so. I went alone and laid my burden before the Lord, praying that, if He wanted me to speak further for China, He would show His will by sending me some gifts that would enable me to get ready-made clothes for the children.

A few days later I was speaking at a Presbyterial gathering in western Ontario. At the close of the evening meeting an old gentleman put into my hands some money. I asked him what he wished me to use it for, and he replied, "For your children. Use it in a way that will help you to be free for God's work." My heart rose in thanksgiving, and I decided to accept it as the token I had asked of the Lord. On my return to Toronto I spent this gift in buying clothes for the children, to save my time and strength for the Lord's work.

When busy in my home one day, the thought of two dear friends of the China Inland Mission kept coming constantly to mind, and I began to wonder if I should not send them some money. Looking into my purse, I found I had only fifty cents on hand. I put the matter out of my mind, with the thought that if the Lord wanted me to send them anything He would provide a way. That afternoon's mail brought a letter from a distant place in Ontario where, a year before, I had visited and spoken for a friend. The letter was from the treasurer of the Christian Endeavor Society for which I had spoken. He enclosed five dollars, and said the money was to have been given me at the time I spoke for them, but had been overlooked.

My first thought was to return it, as it would be dishonoring my friend to accept money for such a service; and then I remembered my friends for whom I wanted money, and I decided to send the five dollars to them. My husband, returning the following morning, handed me another five to put with it, and the ten dollars was sent off.

In due course a reply came from my friends, saying that the very morning my letter arrived they both had been given assurance that a certain sum would come, for which they had been praying. This was to meet a need which they did not wish to bring before their board. My letter brought the ten dollars; and another letter in the afternoon's mail contained a sum which, with mine, exactly made the amount they had been asking the Lord for.

Say not my soul, "Can God relieve my care?"
Remember that Omnipotence hath servants everywhere!

On one occasion, when about to leave home on a ten-day trip to Montreal and other places, word came that the children's Sunday school treat was to take place during my absence.

Little Mary had no "best" dress for the occasion. I had planned to make her a white woolen dress, but now there was no time; and I knew I could not make it while away, with so many meetings ahead. But, that very day, a lady from our church called and said she had wanted for a long time to help me, and asked if she could do any sewing for me. With dim eyes and a grateful heart I accepted her offer. On my return, Mary told me of her wearing a pretty white dress to the Sunday school treat.

Once more we planned to leave Canada for China, and a serious problem faced me. Our eldest son could be left to face the world alone, but not our daughter of sixteen. It was necessary that a suitable guardian be found for her. I called on three different ones whom I thought would feel some responsibility toward the missionary's daughter, but all three declined to accept the responsibility. I then saw that it was not for me to try to open doors, but for this also I must look to the Lord. I prayed that, if He wished me to return to China, He would send me one to whom I could commit her.

A short time passed; then a lady called, whose life had been devoted to the training of young women. Her beautiful Christian character made her the one above all others in whose care I could gladly leave my daughter. This lady told me that in her early years she had hoped to give her life for service in China, but the way had been closed. She now felt that the Lord had laid it upon her heart to offer to take charge of my child. Years have passed since then, and she has fulfilled my highest expectations of her. Rarely has a more definite answer come from a loving Father, nor one that brought greater relief and help; for this offer, coming as it did in answer to my prayers, seemed to be unmistakable proof that the Lord would keep my child as I gave her up.

The time had almost arrived for beginning the last preparations for the long journey to China, when one day Ruth came in from her play with her heavy coat almost in shreds, she having in some way torn it on a barbed wire fence. The coat was the only heavy one she had, and I had planned to make it do for the ocean voyage, intending to get a new one in England. I tried to find a new one in the stores, but the season was past and I could not; and I had no time to make another. I just took the need to the Lord and left it there, believing that in some way He would provide. A few days later a friend telephoned me that her mother had recently returned from a visit to Chicago, and wished me to come over to see a parcel she had brought for me. Oh, the relief that came when I found that the parcel contained, among other things, a handsome red cloth coat, which fitted Ruth perfectly. This fresh evidence of the Lord's overshadowing care touched me deeply. Those who have never known such tokens of the Lord's loving care in the little things of life can scarcely understand the blessedness that such experiences bring.

Whether it be so heavy that others cannot bear
To know the heavy burden they cannot come and
   share;
Whether it be so tiny that others cannot see
Why it should be a burden, and seem so real to me.
Either and both I lay them down at the Master's feet
And find them alone with Jesus mysteriously sweet.

As I attempt to recall the answers to prayer on this furlough, so many come to mind it is impossible to record them all—help in keeping my appointments, courage and power for public speaking, physical strength, and guidance in facing many difficult problems.

It was at this time I formed a habit of getting a message for a meeting on my knees. It often seemed to me very wonderful how, as in a flash, sometimes, an outline for a talk on China would come. Never having kept notes, nor even outlines of addresses, I have frequently been placed in circumstances when I have felt utterly cast on the Lord. And I can testify that He never failed to give the needed help and the realized divine power. Yet sad, sad is it that often at just such times, no sooner would the address be ended than the Satan-whispered thought would come, *I have done well today.*

Oh, is not the goodness and forbearance of our

God wonderful—wonderful that He ever again would deign to give help when asked for it?

A short time since I asked a dear friend whose writings have reached and inspired multitudes throughout the Christian world: "How did you do it?"

Softly, with deep reverence in look and tone, she replied: "It has been done all in and through prayer!"

With deepest gratitude and praise to our ever faithful God, I too can testify that my little service I have been able to do has been done by His grace in answer to prayer.

> I stood amazed and whispered, "Can it be
> That He hath granted all the boon I sought,
> How wonderful that He for me hath wrought!"
>
>   *   *   *

Oh, faithless heart! He *said* that He would hear,
And proved His promise, wherefore didst thou fear?
How wonderful if He should fail to bless
Expectant prayer with good success!

8

Our God of the Impossible

Behold I am the Lord . . . is there anything too hard for me? JEREMIAH 32:27
Ah Lord God! there is nothing too wonderful for thee. JEREMIAH 32:17 (ASV marg.)

The following illustration of the truth, "What is impossible with man is possible with God," occurred while we were attending the Keswick Convention in England in 1910.

One evening my husband returned from an evening meeting, which I had not attended, and told me of a woman who had come to him in great distress. She had been an earnest Christian worker, but love for light, trashy fiction had so grown upon her as to work havoc in her Christian life. She had come to Keswick three years in succession, hoping to get victory, but had failed.

My whole soul went out to the poor woman; I longed to help her. But my husband did not know her name, and the tent had been so dark he could not recognize her again; besides, there were about four thousand people attending the convention.

That night I lay awake asking the Lord, if He knew I could help her, to bring us together, for I too had at one time been almost wrecked on the same rock.

Three evenings later the tent was so crowded that I found difficulty in getting a seat. Just as the meeting was about to begin, I noticed a woman change her seat twice, and then rise a third time and come to where I was, asking me to make room for her. I crowded the others in the seat and made room for her—I fear not too graciously. While Mr. F. B. Meyer was speaking, I noticed she was in great distress, her tears falling fast. I laid my hand on hers, and she grasped it convulsively. At the close of the meeting I said, "Can I help you?"

"Oh, no," she replied, "there is no hope for me; it is those cursed novels that have been my ruin."

I looked at her in amazement and almost gasped: "Are you the one who spoke to Mr. Goforth Sunday night?"

"Yes; but who are you?"

Scarcely able to speak for emotion, I told her, and also of my prayer. For the next few moments we could only weep together. Then the Lord used me to lead the poor crushed and broken soul back to Himself. As we parted, a few days later, her face was beaming with the joy of the Lord.

While addressing a gathering of Christians in Glasgow I was giving a certain incident, the point of which depended upon a verse of a certain hymn. When I came to quote the verse, it had utterly slipped my memory. In some confusion I turned to the leader, hoping that he could help me out; but he said he had no idea what the hymn was. Turning again to the people, I had to acknowledge that my memory had failed me, and, feeling embarrassed, I closed my message somewhat hurriedly.

Sitting down, I lifted my heart in a cry to the Lord to lead me to the verse I wanted, if it was in the hymnbook used there. I took up a hymnbook and opened it, and the very first lines my eyes fell on were those of the verse I wanted, though it was the last verse of a long hymn. Rising again, I told the people of my prayer and the answer, and gave them the verse. The solemn stillness which prevailed indicated that a deep impression had been made. Some two years after, a newly arrived missionary in China told me he had been present at that meeting, and how this little incident had been a great blessing to him. "They cried unto thee, and were delivered: they trusted in thee, and were not confounded" (Ps 22:5).

Before leaving Canada we had written to the China Inland School at Chefoo, China, hoping to get our children admitted there; but, shortly before we left England for China, word reached us that both the boys' and girls' schools were overflowing, with long lists of waiting applicants. This was a great blow to me, for I had been looking forward to engaging once more in the aggressive outstation work.

But the children could not be left, and were too old to be taken away from their studies. It seemed necessary, therefore, that a good Christian governess should be found, who would teach the children

96

and take charge of the home in my absence. All the way across the Siberian route this matter was before us. Earnestly did I pray that the Lord would direct the right one to us; for I knew that to get a young woman, who could fill the position we wanted her for, would be very difficult in China.

We had planned to go direct to our station, but illness forced us to break the journey at Peitaiho, where we met a young lady, the daughter of a missionary. Many difficulties appeared in the way of her coming on with us, but one by one these were removed; and when we continued our journey this young woman was one of our party.

Time proved her to be truly God-given. Not only was she all and more than I could have hoped for, but the Lord answered my prayers that her young life might be consecrated to the Lord's service in China. She later went through her training in England as a nurse, and then to China as a missionary of the China Inland Mission.

The summer holidays at Peitaiho were drawing to a close. Heavy rains had fallen, making the roads to the station, six miles distant, almost impassable. Word had come that our two children, Ruth and Wallace, must leave by the Monday morning train in order to reach the steamer at Tientsin, which was to take them to Chefoo, where they were attending the China Inland Mission schools. All day Saturday and Sunday torrents of rain continued to fall, with a fierce wind from the north.

I rose before daybreak Monday morning, to find

the rain still pouring down in torrents. I roused
the servant, and sent him off to make sure about
the chair, cart, and donkeys. A little later he returned to say that the chair had been blown over,
and the chair-bearers had refused to come. The
carters also refused, saying the roads were impassable; and even the donkey boys said they would
not go.

I was truly at wit's end; I went alone, and did
not take time even to kneel down, but just lifted
up my heart to my Father to stop the rain and open
a way for the children to get to the station. I felt
a sudden, strong confidence that the Lord would
help, and, going out again, I ordered the servant to
run fast to the village nearby and get fresh donkeys.
He was unwilling, saying it was useless, no one
would venture; but I said, "Go at once, I know
they will come."

While he was gone the children had their breakfast, boxes were closed and taken out, and the
children put on their wraps. Then the rain stopped!
Just then the servant returned with several donkeys.
Within five minutes, children and baggage were on
donkeys, and started for the station. A few hours
later one of the donkey boys returned with a hastily
written note from Ruth, saying they had reached
the station without any mishap and quite dry; for
it had not rained on the way over, but had started
to pour again just after they had got on the train.
The rain continued for days after.

At the close of our four months of meetings in
Great Britain, in 1910, I felt a strong desire to send

a gift of five dollars to five Christian works in Britain, to show in a practical way our sympathy with the workers in these various branches of the Lord's work.

My husband was in the midst of his accounts when I asked him to give me five pounds for this purpose. He told me it was impossible, as we had barely enough for the journey to China. As I left him I wondered why I seemed to have these gifts so definitely laid upon me to send, when there was no money. Reasoning that if the thing were really of the Lord He could Himself give me what He wished me to send, I put that matter from my mind.

That evening's mail brought a letter from a stranger living some distance away, judging from the postmark; for the letter had no address, and was not signed. The letter said:

"I do not know you, nor have I met you, but the Lord seems to have laid it on my heart to send you this five-pound note as a farewell gift. Do what you think best with it."

It was with a joyful heart I sent off the gifts to the five Christian workers in Britain. Had the giver said it was "for work in China," as was usually the case, I could not have used it for any other purpose.

How to get the sewing done for my family and yet meet the pressing calls made upon me as the wife of a pioneer missionary, for almost thirty years has been perhaps the most difficult and constant problem of my missionary life. In connection with the solving of this problem, I have seen some of the most precious evidences of God's willingness to undertake in the daily details of life.

The following story must be given in detail to be really understood, as one of the striking instances of how God, in His own wonderful way, can work out the seemingly impossible.

Returning home to our station from an unusually strenuous autumn's touring, I planned as usual to give the month of December to the children's sewing, so as to leave January largely free for a Bible women's training class. But my health broke down, and I could make scarcely any headway with the thirty-five or forty garments which had to be made or fixed over, before the children returned to their school in Chefoo. By December 18 we decided to cancel the class on account of my ill-health; and to all the women, except one whom I entirely forgot, I sent word not to come.

As the days passed, the burden of the almost untouched sewing became very great. At last I cried to the Lord to undertake for me. And how wonderfully He did! On December 28, when I was conducting the Chinese women's prayer meeting, I noticed in the audience Mrs. Lu, the very woman to whom I had forgotten to send word. She had come a long distance, with her little child, over rough mountainous roads, so I felt very sorry for my thoughtlessness. Mrs. Lu accompanied me home, and I gave her money for a barrow on which to return the next day. I then sat down to the sewing machine. The woman stood beside me for a little, and then said,

"You are looking very tired, Mrs. Goforth; let me run the machine for you."

"You!" I exclaimed, astonished. "Why, you don't know how."

"Yes, I do," she replied.

She was so insistent that at last, in fear and trembling, I ventured to let her try—for I had only one needle. It took but a few moments to convince me she was a real expert at the machine. When I urged her to stay and help me, she replied that since the class was given up she would return home on the morrow.

That night I was puzzled. Why should the Lord lead this woman to me—the only one, so far as we knew, who could do the machine work—and then permit her to leave? I could only lay the whole matter before the Lord and trust Him to undertake. And again He answered. That night a fierce storm came on, lasting several days and making the roads quite impassable. Mrs. Lu, finding herself storm-tied, gladly gave all her time to me. The roads remained impassable for a whole month, during which time I did not once need to sit down at the machine.

While in Tientsin with my children during the revolution in 1912, I had occasion to go into the Chinese city with my servant. We visited three stores. On our way home by the tramway, I discovered I had lost a five-dollar bill and one of my gloves. I had foolishly put the bill inside the glove. Ashamed to let the Chinese servant know of my carelessness, I sent him home when we reached the end of the tram line. As soon as he was out of sight I took the tram back to the city. On the way I confessed to the Lord my carelessness and asked Him to keep the glove and money and lead me to where they were. I retraced my steps back to two of the stores where we had been. As I entered the second, which was a shoestore, a number of men were in the shop; but there, right in sight of all, on the floor lay my glove, and I knew of course with the five dollars inside. It was with a heart full of gratitude to my loving heavenly Father, and an enlarged vision of His love, that I picked up the glove and returned home that day.

On one occasion when on furlough with several little children, and my husband in China, I had no settled home. When the time came to do the sewing for the long journey back to China, I had simply no way to get it done. I just had to look to the Lord; and, as so often before, He was again faithful, and opened the way. When shopping downtown one day, I met a minister's wife from a distant country charge, who said, "I want you to come with me with all your children, and get your sewing done. A number of the ladies of our congregation sew well, and will be delighted to help you."

I gratefully accepted her invitation, and while staying with her a sewing bee was held in the church. In one week the sewing was finished, which would have taken me many weeks of hard, constant labor to accomplish alone.

The winter of our return from China, after the Boxer tragedies, I felt keenly the need of a good sewing machine, as I could not possibly do the children's sewing by hand and still get time for meetings. One day, as my husband was leaving on a deputation tour, I asked him for money for a machine. He assured me it was impossible, that we had only sufficient for bare necessities. I knew well he would gladly give me money for the machine if he had it. So I laid my need before my Father, confident that He knew it was a real need, and that according to His promise He could and would supply it.

I was so sure that somehow the money would come, that I went downtown especially to choose a suitable machine. I found it would cost thirty-six dollars. A few days later I received a letter from a band of ladies in Mount Forest, Ontario, enclosing twenty-three dollars and some odd cents, and saying: "Please accept the enclosed to buy something you have lost as our substitute in China." Only a day or two later another letter came, from quite anther part of Ontario, enclosing twelve dollars and some cents. The two amounts came to exactly the sum I needed to purchase the machine.

The second letter stated that the money was sent to help me buy a sewing machine. It has always been a puzzle to me how they came to send the money in that way, for I had not spoken to anyone but my husband about wanting a machine. When Mr. Goforth returned I was able to show him what the Lord could give me, though he could not.

I had been holding a class for women at an outstation, staying in the home of the elder, Dr. Fan.

The day before I was to return home, Mrs. Fan asked me to go with her to visit a very sick boy whom the missionary doctor had sent home from the boy's school, Wei Hwei, because of his having tuberculosis. Mrs. Fan told me the mother was in great distress, and begged me to come and pray with her. I found the lad in a truly pitiable condition. His mouth was swollen, his face a ghastly hue, and every moment a cough racked his frame. He seemed to me quite beyond hope and looked as if he could not live long.

On our way home to Mrs. Fan's, the message of James 5:14-15 kept coming persistently to me, as if spoken by a voice: "Is any sick among you? let him call for the elders of the church; and let them pray over him . . . and the prayer of faith shall save the sick, and the Lord shall raise him up."

I simply could not get away from those words. On reaching Dr. Fan's home, I sent for him, and asked if he and the other elders would be willing to pray with me over the lad. He consented, though at first he seemed rather dubious. There were quite a number of Christians gathered around as we placed the boy in our midst. All knelt down, and I read the words from James. I told them plainly that I could not say that it was indeed the Lord's will to heal the boy; all that was clear to me was that we must obey as far as we had light and leave the rest in God's hands for life or death. Several prayed, and we then dispersed.

Early the following morning I left for home. Circumstances prevented my return to that place, and in time we moved to another field. More than two years later, while visiting Wei Hwei, I met Mrs. Fan, who told me that the lad had completely recovered and was then working with his father. Still a year later I met Dr. Fan, and upon inquiring about the lad, the doctor told me he was perfectly well and was in business in Wei Hwei City.

The power of intercession is shown in the following two incidents:

In the winter of 1905 a call came for my husband to hold special meetings in Manchuria. On reaching Liao Yang for these meetings, one of the missionaries showed him a letter from Mr. Moffat, of Korea, which said, "I have a thousand Christians here who have promised to pray for Mr. Goforth, and I know their prayers will prevail with God." Can we doubt that their prayers had something to do with the marvelous revival movement which followed?

When in England, in 1909, my husband was the guest of a lady in London who was noted for her power in intercession. He was telling her of the great revival movements he had been through, which took place in different provinces in China; and she asked him to look at her diary, in which were notes of times when she had been led out in special intercession for Mr. Goforth. These dates exactly corresponded to the times of greatest revival power.

A few months after we returned to China from a furlough, I invited a certain missionary and his wife and children to pay us a visit. Peculiarly touching circumstances had led me to give this invitation. Both husband and wife were in ill health and greatly needed a change. They resided in a far inland station, quite cut off from other missionaries. They were not connected with any society, and were looking only to the Lord for their support. Just as these friends had started toward us, on their five-day journey, smallpox broke out at our station, and one of the missionaries died. A telegram was sent, hoping to catch them before they left, but it did not reach them until they were a short distance from our station. Then the whole family had to turn around, and once more take the long, trying journey, homeward. As the weather was very cold at the time, one could imagine what a terrible trial to faith the whole experience meant to them. I felt so deeply for them that I planned to send sufficient to cover at least the expense of the journey. But, on getting out of quarantine, I found I could not draw on our treasurer for the fifty dollars needed, as Mr. Goforth was not at home. However, the Lord had seen the need long before I felt it and had the exact amount ready. Three days after I got out of quarantine, I received a letter from Mr. Horace Goven, of the Faith Mission, Glasgow, enclosing a draft for five pounds which, at the rate of exchange at that time, came to fifty dollars Mexican. The gift came from the workers of the mission, and he stated that they wished me to accept it as a personal gift. Needless to say, the draft was sent off the same day to the needy friends in the far-off station.

On one ocassion, while we were temporarily stationed at Wei Hwei, Honan, I was called to nurse a fellow missionary who had contracted black small-pox. This missionary died; and it was while shut away from everyone during the time of quarantine that I had the following experience:

I awoke suddenly one night feeling greatly troubled for one in Canada. So strong was the impression that this friend needed my prayers, that I felt compelled to rise and spend a long time wrestling with God on this one's behalf; then peace came, and I again slept.

As soon as I was out of quarantine, I wrote to my friend and told of this experience, giving the date. In time the answer came, which said that— though no date could be given, as no note had been made of it—as far as could be judged, it was about the same time that I had had the burden of prayer that my friend was passing through a time of such temptation as seemed almost overwhelming. But the letter said: "I was brought through victoriously; I know that it was your prayers that helped me."

The following incident may seem trifling to some, but to me no answer in my life ever brought more intense relief. For this reason I have reserved it, as the final testimony of the original prayer record.

My husband had gone to hold revival meetings in a distant province, and while he was away I went with my Bible women to a certain outstation at the urgent request of the Christians, to preach at four-day "theatrical," which brought great crowds. The four days there were enough to wear out the strongest; for many hours daily we had to face unruly crowds coming and going; and at the end of our stay I turned my face homeward utterly worn out. My one thought was to get to Wei Hwei, our next station, for a few days' rest with my youngest children, who were attending school there. A sight of them, I knew, would recover my energies better than anything else.

But in getting home I, in some way, lost the key of the money-drawer. It was Friday, and the train for Wei Hwei left on Saturday at ten o'clock. Different persons came for money, but I had to put them off with some excuse. There was too much money in the drawer for me to leave with the key lying around somewhere; besides, I myself could not go without money.

As soon as I had my supper, I started searching everywhere. Drawers, pigeonholes, shelves were all searched in vain. After hunting for two hours, until I was too exhausted to hunt anymore, I suddenly thought, *I have never prayed about it.* Stopping still just where I stood by the dining room table, I lifted my heart to the Lord. "O Lord, You know how much I need a rest; You know how much I long to see the children; pity me, and lead me to the key."

Then, without wasting a step, I walked through the dining room, hall, and women's guestroom into my husband's study, to the bookcase (which covers one side of the room), opened the door, slipped two books aside, and there was the key. So near did the Lord seem at that moment that I could almost feel

His bodily presence. It was not that I remembered
putting the key there, but He led me there.

Yes, I *know* God answers prayer.

9

To His Praise!

They shall abundantly utter the memory of thy great goodness. PSALM 145:7

This chapter is written more than seven years later than the foregoing, in further testimony and praise.

Returning to Canada at the time of World War I, we came face to face with a serious financial crisis. Only two ways seemed open to us. One was to lay our affairs frankly before the Board, showing that our salary was quite insufficient, with war conditions and prices, to meet our requirements. The other course was to just go forward, get a suitable home and whatever we required, and trust our Father to supply what was needed above our income. We decided on the latter course.

My dear daughter felt indignant that we should have a salary insufficient for our needs; but we assured her that to trust God for what was lacking was not begging. The day came when this child and myself took possession of our new home. As we entered the dining room we found a large mail from China on the table.

One letter was forwarded from the lady in Australia whose gifts, in the past, seemed always to have met some felt need. Her letter enclosed fifty pounds, with the expressed wish that thirty pounds should be used for work in China, but twenty pounds was to be used to meet some personal need. I handed the letter to my daughter, saying, "Shall we not believe that God will undertake for us? It seems to me as if our Father were beside us saying, 'My child, take this hundred dollars as an earnest of what I am going to do for you.'"

Tears stood in her eyes as my daughter gave the letter back, saying, "Mother, we don't trust God half enough!"

Were I to attempt to write the history of the months that followed, a long chapter would be required; but my testimony along this line is surely sufficient.

It was on this same furlough that I came to have an enlarged vision of my heavenly Father's willingness to undertake in what some might term the minor details of everyday life. Missionaries, especially we missionary women, know only too well how we are criticized in the matter of dress, when in the homeland and when traveling. I have had, through the years, not only many amusing but trying experiences in this connection, and I resolved to make the question of dress a definite matter of prayer. And I rejoice to testify that the result of this decision became a constant source of wonder and praise. Yes, I found the Lord could guide me even in trimming my hat to His glory! That is, so that I could stand up before an audience and not bring discredit to my Master. Praise His name!

> There is nothing too great for His power,
> And nothing too small for His love!

At the time of World War I a son had gone to England with the first Canadian contingent. When this news reached us in China, I began to pray definitely that the Lord would use my son's gifts in the best way for his country's good, but would keep him back from the trenches and from actual warfare. My boy did not know of this prayer.

Some weeks after reaching England, he was looking forward to leaving for the trenches in France, when orders came that he was needed in the orderly room, and his unit left without him. Months later a call came for volunteers, to fill the great gaps made at the time of the first use of gas. My boy resigned his position and joined the company of volunteers to be sent to France. Just before they were to leave he was again sent for from headquarters and told he was to go to the Canadian base in France as adjutant. His duties in this capacity kept him at the forwarding base. A year later he again planned to resign in order to get to the trenches. He had begun making arrangements for this step, when he fell from his horse, which caused him to be invalided home to Canada, where he was kept till the close of the war.

It would indeed be difficult to persuade his mother that all this happened by chance; for one day, when in great distress, expecting any day a cable to say he had left for the trenches, I received a clear assurance from the Lord that he had the boy in His keeping.

After our return to China, when in great trouble, I prayed the Lord to grant me a clear sign of His favor by giving me a certain petition, which affected a child in the homeland. The request was a complicated one, including several definite details. A little more than a month later, a letter reached me from the one for whom I had asked the Lord's favor. She wrote joyously, telling that she had received just what I had asked for, and in every detail as I had prayed.

When my husband resigned the regular field work of Changte, Honan, it became necessary for us to find a home elsewhere. The only suitable place, meeting all our requirements, was on the hills at Kikungshan, South Honan. On going there to get a site for our home, though we looked for more than a week, we could find no place. As we started down the hill, one morning soon after midnight, I was feeling our failure very keenly, for we had given up our old home. When my husband saw how bad I felt, as he told me later, he began to cry earnestly to the Lord to give us a site. And before we reached the station the assurance had come that we would get a place. A friend on the train, traveling third class, saw us getting on the second class, and came in for a few words before getting off the train. When he heard we had failed to get a site, he said, "I know of a beautiful site which our mission is reserving for a future missionary. I'll ask them to give it to you."

A few days later the treasurer of this mission wrote us that they had unanimously and gladly voted to give us the site.

I am now writing these closing words in our God-given home, built on this beautiful site, one of the loveliest spots to be found in China. So from this quiet mountain retreat, a monument of what God can give in answer to prayer, this little book of prayer testimonies is sent forth.

As the past has been reviewed, and God's wonderful faithfulness recalled, there has come a great sense of regret that I have not trusted God more and asked more of Him, both for my family and the Chinese. Yes, it is truly wonderful! But the wonder is not that God *can* answer prayer, *but that He does,* when we so imperfectly meet the conditions clearly laid down in His Word.

In recent years I have often tested myself by these conditions, when weeks, and perhaps months, have passed without some answer to prayer, and there has come a conscious spiritual sagging. As the discerning soul can plainly see, all the conditions mentioned in the list below may be included in the one word *Abide.*

Conditions of Prevailing Prayer

1. Contrite humility before God and forsaking of sin—2 Chronicles 7:14.

2. Seeking God with the whole heart—Jeremiah 29:12-13.

3. Faith in God—Mark 11:23-24.

4. Obedience—1 John 3:22.

5. Dependence on the Holy Spirit—Romans 8:26.

6. Importunity—Mark 7:24-30; Luke 11:5-10.

7. Must ask in accordance with God's will—1 John 5:14.

8. In Christ's name—John 14:13-14, and many other passages.

9. Must be willing to make amends for wrongs to others—Matthew 5:23-24.

CAUSES OF FAILURE IN PRAYER

1. Sin in the heart and life—Psalm 66:18; Isaiah 59:1-2.

2. Persistent refusal to obey God—Proverbs 1:24-28; Zechariah 7:11,13.

3. Formalism and hypocrisy—Isaiah 1:2-15.

4. Unwillingness to forgive others—Mark 11:25-26.

5. Wrong motives—James 4:2-3.

6. Despising God's law—Amos 2:4.

7. Lack of love and mercy—Proverbs 21:13.

10

Victory Found

At the close of this little volume it seems fitting to recount again a wonderful personal experience, narrated in *The Sunday School Times* of December 7, 1918.

I do not remember the time when I did not have in some degree a love for the Lord Jesus Christ as my Saviour. When not quite twelve years of age, at a revival meeting, I publicly accepted and confessed Christ as my Lord and Master.

From that time there grew up in my heart a deep yearning to know Christ in a more real way, for He seemed so unreal, so far away and visionary. One night when still quite young I remember going out under the trees in my parents' garden and, looking up into the starlit heavens, I longed with intense longing to feel Christ near me. As I knelt down there on the grass, alone with God, Job's cry became mine, "Oh, that I knew where I might find him!" Could I have borne it had I known then that almost forty years would pass before that yearning would be satisfied?

With the longing to know Christ, literally to "find" Him, came a passionate desire to *serve* Him. But, oh, what a terrible nature I had! Passionate, proud, self-willed, indeed just full was I of those things that I knew were unlike Christ.

The following years of halfhearted conflict with sinful self must be passed over till about the fifth year of our missionary work in China. I grieve to say that the new life in a foreign land with its trying climate, provoking servants, and altogether irritating conditions, seemed to have developed rather than subdued my natural disposition.

One day (I can never forget it), as I sat inside the house by a paper window at dusk, two Chinese Christian women sat down on the other side. They began talking about me, and (wrongly, no doubt) I listened. One said, "Yes, she is a hard worker, a zealous preacher, and—yes, she dearly loves us; but, oh, what a temper she has! *If she would only live more as she preaches!*"

Then followed a full and true delineation of my life and character. So true indeed was it, as to crush out all sense of annoyance and leave me humbled to the dust. I saw then how useless, how worse than useless, was it for me to come to China to preach Christ and not *live* Christ. But how could I live Christ? I knew some (including my dear husband) who had a peace and a power—yes, and a something I could not define—that I had not; and often I longed to know the secret.

Was it possible, with such a nature as mine, ever to become patient and gentle?

Was it possible that I could ever really stop worrying?

Could I, in a word, ever hope to be able to live Christ as well as preach Him?

I knew I loved Christ; and again and again I had proved my willingness to give up all for His sake. But I knew, too, that one hot flash of temper with the Chinese or with the children before the Chinese, would largely undo weeks, perhaps months, of self-sacrificing service.

The years that followed led often through the furnace. The Lord knew that nothing but fire could destroy the dross and subdue my stubborn will. Those years may be summed up in one line: "Fighting [not finding], following, keeping, *struggling*." Yes, and failing! Sometimes in the depths of despair over these failures; then going on determined to do *my* best—and what a poor best it was!

In the year 1905, and later, as I witnessed the wonderful way the Lord was leading my husband and saw the Holy Spirit's power in his life and message, I came to seek very definitely for the fullness of the Holy Spirit. It was a time of deep heart-searching. The heinousness of sin was revealed as never before. Many, many things had to be set right toward man and God. I learned then what "paying the price" meant. Those were times of wonderful mountaintop experiences, and I came to honor the Holy Spirit and seek His power for the overcoming of sin in a new way. But Christ still remained, as before, distant, afar off, and I longed increasingly to know—to *find* Him. Although I had much more power over besetting sins, yet there were times of great darkness and defeat.

It was during one of these latter times that we were forced to return to Canada, in June 1916. My husband's health prevented him from public speaking, and it seemed that this duty for us both was to fall on me. But I dreaded facing the home church without spiritual uplift—a fresh vision for myself. The Lord saw this heart hunger, and in His own glorious way He fulfilled literally the promise, "He satisfieth the longing soul, and *filleth* the hungry soul with goodness" (Ps 107:9).

A spiritual conference was to be held the latter part of June at Niagara-on-the-Lake, Ontario, and to this I was led. One day I went to the meeting rather against my inclination, for it was so lovely under the trees by the beautiful lake. The speaker was a stranger to me, but from almost the first his message gripped me—"Victory over Sin!" Why, this was what I had fought for, had hungered for, all my life! Was it possible?

The speaker went on to describe very simply an ordinary Christian life experience—sometimes on the mountaintop, with visions of God; then again would come the sagging and dimming of vision, coldness, discouragement, and perhaps definite disobedience, and a time of downgrade experience. Then perhaps a sorrow, or even some special mercy, would bring the wanderer back to his Lord.

The speaker asked for all those who felt this to be a picture of their experience to raise the hand. I was sitting in the front seat, and shame only kept me from raising my hand at once. But I did so want to get all God had for me, and I determined to be true; and after a struggle I raised my hand. Wondering if others were like myself, I ventured to glance back and saw many hands were raised, though the audience was composed almost entirely of Christian workers, ministers, and missionaries.

The leader then went on to say *that* life which he had described was *not* the life God planned or wished for His children. He described the higher life of peace, rest in the Lord, of power and freedom from struggle, worry, care. As I listened I could scarcely believe it could be true, yet my whole soul was moved so that it was with the greatest difficulty I could control my emotion. I saw then, though dimly, that I was nearing the goal for which I had been aiming all my life.

Early the next morning, soon after daybreak, on my knees I went over carefully and prayerfully all the passages on the victorious life that were given in a little leaflet. What a comfort and strength it was to see how clear God's Word was that victory, not defeat, was His will for His children, and to see what wonderful provision He had made! Later, during the days that followed, clearer light came. I did what I was asked to do—I quietly but definitely accepted Christ as my Saviour from the *power* of sin as I had so long before accepted Him as my Saviour from the *penalty* of sin. And on this I rested.

I left Niagara, realizing, however, there was still

something I did not have. I felt much as the blind man must have felt when he said, "I see men as trees, walking." I had begun to see light, but dimly.

The day after reaching home I picked up a little booklet, *The Life That Wins,* which I had not read before, and going to my son's bedside I told him it was the personal testimony of one whom God had used to bring great blessing into my life. I then read it aloud till I came to the words, "At last I realized that Jesus Christ was actually and literally within me." I stopped amazed. The sun seemed suddenly to come from under a cloud and flood my whole soul with light. How blind I had been! I saw at last the secret of victory—it was simply Jesus Christ Himself—His own life lived out in the believer. But the thought of victory was for the moment lost sight of in the inexpressible joy of realizing *Christ's indwelling presence!* Like a tired, worn-out wanderer finding home at last I just *rested* in Him. Rested in His love—in Himself. And, oh, the peace and joy that came flooding my life! A restfulness and quietness of spirit I never thought could be mine took possession of me so naturally. Literally a new life began for me, or rather *in* me. It was just "the life that is Christ."

The first step I took in this new life was to stand on God's own Word and not merely on man's teaching or even on a personal experience. And as I studied especially the truth of God's indwelling, victory over sin, and God's bountiful provision, the Word was fairly illuminated with new light.

The years that have passed have been years of blessed fellowship with Christ and of joy in His service. A friend asked me not long ago if I could give in a sentence the after-result in my life of what I said had come to me in 1916, and I replied, "Yes, it can be all summed up in one word: *resting*."

Some have asked, "But have you never sinned?" Yes, I grieve to say I have. Sin is the one thing I abhor—for it is the one thing that can, if unrepented of, separate us, not only from Christ, but from the consciousness of His presence. But I have learned that there is instantaneous forgiveness and restoration to be had *always*. There need be no times of despair.

One of the blessed results of this life is not only the consciousness of Christ's presence, but the *reality* of His presence as manifested in definite results when, in the daily details of life, matters are left with Him and He has undertaken.

My own thought of Him is beautifully expressed in Spurgeon's words:

> What the hand is to the lute,
> What the breath is to the flute,
> What's the mother to the child,
> What the guide in pathless wild,
> What is oil to troubled wave,
> What is ransom to a slave,
> What is flower to the bee,
>   That is Jesus Christ to me.

The special Bible study which I made at that time is added below.

The secret of victory is simply Christ Himself in the heart of the believer. This truth of Christ's indwelling is and always has been a *mystery*.

Romans 16:25
Ephesians 3:9 with Colossians 1:26-27
Ephesians 5:30, 32 (ASV)
Colossians 4:3

Christ Himself taught this truth.

John 14:20, 23; 15:1-7; 17:21-23
Matthew 28:20
Revelation 3:20 (See also Mk 16:20)

It was a vital reality to the apostle Paul.

Romans 8:10
1 Corinthians 6:15
1 Corinthians 12:27 (ASV)
2 Corinthians 5:17
2 Corinthians 13:5
Galatians 2:20
Galatians 3:27
Galatians 4:19
Ephesians 3:17
Philippians 1:21
1 Thessalonians 5:10
Hebrews 3:6

The words *in Christ,* which recur in many other passages, will have a new literalness when read in the light of the above.

The apostle John had a like conception of Christ's indwelling presence.

1 John 2:28—3:6, 24
1 John 4:4, 12, 13, 16
1 John 5:20

GOD'S PURPOSE

As victory is the result of Christ's life lived out in the believer, it is important that we see clearly that *victory,* and not *defeat,* is God's purpose for His children. The Scriptures are very decided upon this truth.

Luke 1:74-75
Romans 5:2
Romans 6 and 8 (Ro 7 should be read in the
     light of Ro 6 and 8)
1 Corinthians 15:57
2 Corinthians 2:14
2 Corinthians 10:5
Ephesians 1:3-4
Colossians 4:12
1 Thessalonians 5:23
2 Thessalonians 3:3 (ASV)
2 Timothy 2:19
Titus 2:12
Hebrews 7:25
1 Peter 1:15
2 Peter 3:14
1 John 2:1
1 John 3:6, 9
          And many other passages.

That Christ came as the Saviour from the *power* as well as the *penalty* of sin we see in Matthew 1:21, with John 8:34, 36, and Titus 2:14.

GOD'S PROVISION

God knew the frailty of man, that his heart was "desperately wicked," that even his righteousness was "as filthy rags," that man's only hope for victory over sin must come from the Godward side. He therefore made kingly provision so rich, so sufficient, so exceeding abundant, that as we study it we feel we have tapped a mine of wealth too deep to fathom. Just a few suggestions of its riches:

God's *greatest* provision is the gift of a part of His own being in the Person of the Holy Spirit. The following are about some of the many things the Holy Spirit does for us, as recorded in the Word:

He begets us into the family of God—John 3:6.

He seals or marks us as God's—Ephesians 1:13.

He dwells in us—1 Corinthians 3:16.

He unites us to Christ—1 Corinthians 12:13, 27.

He changes us into the likeness of Christ—2 Corinthians 3:18.

He helps in prayer—Romans 8:26.

He comforts—John 14:16.

He guides—Romans 8:14.

He strengthens with power—Ephesians 3:16.

He is the source of power and fruitfulness—John 7:38-39.

Some of the victorious *results* in our life, as Christ has His way in us, are shown in:

Romans 8:32, 37
Romans 15:13
2 Corinthians 9:8, 11
2 Corinthians 2:14
Ephesians 1:19
Ephesians 3:16, 20
Philippians 4:7, 13, 19
Colossians 1:11
1 Peter 1:5
2 Timothy 3:17
Jude 24
John 15:7

To the seeker for further scripture help, I would suggest a plan that has proved a great blessing to me.

Read the Psalms through, making careful record of all the statements of what the Lord was to the writers of the Psalms. The list will surprise you. Then on your knees go over them one by one, with the prayer that Christ may be to you what He was to David and the others.

Take a Cruden's, or, better still, a Young's concordance, and look up the texts under such headings as Love, Fullness, Power, Riches, and Grace, grouping them into usable Bible studies. As a sample, taking this last word, *Grace;* the more one studies it the more wonderful does it become. Here are some of these headings:

Grace for grace—John 1:16.

Sufficient grace—2 Corinthians 12:9.

More grace—James 4:6.

All grace—2 Corinthians 9:8.

Abundant grace—Romans 5:17.

Exceeding abundant grace—1 Timothy 1:14.

Exceeding riches of His grace—Ephesians 2:17.

But let us remember that to know simply of riches will never materially benefit us. We must make them our own. All fullness dwells in Christ. It is only as we "apprehend" (which means take hold or take in) Christ through the Holy Spirit can it be possible for these spiritual riches to become ours. The slogan of this glorious life in Christ is just, "Let go and let God."